T5-DIJ-670

THE WORLD CAR :
The Future of the Automobile Industry

THE WORLD CAR :
The Future of the Automobile Industry

Stuart Sinclair

FACTS ON FILE PUBLICATIONS
460 Park Avenue South, New York, N.Y. 10016

338. 476292
S 61 w

THE WORLD CAR

The Future of the Automobile Industry

Copyright © 1983 Euromonitor Publications Limited.

Published by Facts On File, Inc., 460 Park Avenue South,
New York, N.Y. 10016

All rights reserved. No part of this book may be reproduced
in any form whatever without the express written consent
of the publisher except for reasonably brief extracts used
in reviews or scholarly works.

Library of Congress Cataloging in Publication Data

Sinclair, Stuart W.
  The world car.

  Bibliography: p.
  Includes index.
  1. Automobile industry and trade.   2. Automobile
industry and trade — International cooperation.
3. International division of labor.   I. Title.
HD.9710.A2S56 1983   338.4'76292   82-24173
ISBN 0-87196-285-3

Printed and bound in the United Kingdom

CONTENTS

OCT 13 '83

UNIVERSITY LIBRARIES
CARNEGIE-MELLON UNIVERSITY
PITTSBURGH, PENNSYLVANIA 15213

LIST OF TABLES IN TEXT

LIST OF CHARTS IN TEXT

STATISTICAL SUPPLEMENT

List of Tables

STATISTICAL SUPPLEMENT : List of Tables continued ...

STATISTICAL SUPPLEMENT : List of Tables continued ...

Chapter One

Introduction

Issues for the 1980s

There is no doubt that the car industry is among the most important in the world. An increasing number of governments, most recently the French, are according it the status of a key or spearhead industry, to be preserved and — if possible — rejuvenated at all costs. In the face of growing exports from Japan, many governments hitherto more or less committed to the principles of free trade in manufactured goods are also moving to protect the car firms within their borders. Now even West Germany, the last major car manufacturing country in the west to set ceilings on Japanese import penetration, has followed the line set earlier in the decade by the USA, and years before by Italy, France, the UK and others. Elsewhere in the world, many developing country governments are becoming increasingly involved in the car industry too, seeing it as a crucial leading sector capable of throwing off linkages to a range of other domestic suppliers and of taking a leading role in the industrialization process in the economy at large.

The figures bear out these governments' perceptions of the industry's importance. By the early 1980s international trade in fully assembled cars was accounting for around 7% of the value of all international trade — which in 1981 totalled $2,000 billion[1]. The total value of car output was equivalent to 8.8% of all manufacturing output in the developed countries in 1975 (having risen from 8.2% in 1963), while in COMECON countries it was 7.2% in 1975, having fallen from 7.9% in 1963. For a sample of 18 developed countries (generally the more advanced among them) the share of transport equipment in total manufacturing output in 1963 was 4.0%. By 1975 (with 43 countries in the sample) it was 4.8%[2].

As far as employment is concerned, the auto industry is even more significant than the output figures might suggest. In the USA, even the number laid off after 1980 is large: GM alone had 125,000 hourly workers on indefinite layoff early in 1982. During 1979, 1980 and 1981, Ford and Chrysler had gone further than this, closing 14 plants between them, with a total of 34,000 hourly and salaried staff laid off. In the 1980-82 period Chrysler's hourly paid labour force alone fell by 20,000. Among the EEC members (excluding Greece) car firms employ 6.9% of all manufacturing workers, or 1,954,000 people. In France and Germany the share is particularly high, at 9%. Although the share of car employment in total employment has, naturally, fluctuated over the past, it has tended to remain within the 6-7% range during

---

1. Billions are defined, in the American style, as thousands of millions.
2. UNIDO, *World Industry in 1980* (UN: New York, 1981).

the past ten years. The lowest ratio reached recently was 5.9%, in 1975. Despite this appearance of overall stability, some car-producing countries have seen employment fall substantially. The worst European case of this is the UK. In 1971 the major car firms there employed 304,000 people. By early 1982, employment in the car industry stood at only 196,000 and impending further job cuts at Ford and BL will reduce this figure by another 10,000 or so by the end of the year. Moreover, the pace at which British car industry jobs have been disappearing has been growing. Within the total of 108,000 jobs lost over the 1971-81 period, a full 39,000 of them disappeared in 1981 alone.

Although the importance of the industry today is beyond question, what is far less well-established is the future of the industry. As long ago as the 1960s critics were expressing doubts as to whether the private car would survive as a major means of transport even into the 1980s. The congestion and pollution it engendered would, it was argued, soon grow too much for societies to tolerate. Indeed, a glance at the urban planning and transport planning literature from many countries confirms that identifying and costing the disadvantages of private use has tended always to be, and indeed remains, a major preoccupation. In retrospect it can be seen that "it was about 1966 that town planners realised that unrestrained car growth would bring cities to a halt"[1]. As environmental and social cost arguments began to gather ground in many developed countries, policy came to reflect these new priorities. "Perhaps the single factor most responsible for the rapid growth of the transit program has been the growing strength of anti-highway sentiment among liberals and "good government" supporters generally"[1]. Denser traffic, particularly insofar as it restricts pedestrians' freedom to roam, came to be seen as a "social cost which represents an erosion of progress towards equity"[2]. This argument went on to assert that "safe and convenient access needs to be seen as a basic right of the population . . ." and thus, "public policy (should) accept that it is not necessarily in the public interest to increase dependence on cars"[3].

Accompanying this trend in official and academic thinking was the increasing interest of journalists and critics in transport affairs. Such best-selling works as *The Greening of America* and *Future Shock* referred to the horrors caused by the unconstrained growth of private car ownership. Others concentrated on the idea of the irrationality created by the car. In *Paradise Lost: The Decline of the Auto-Industrial Age,* Emma Rothschild forecast how, in the next two decades, "the real cost of the present and historical structure of automotive support will become ever more evident and disruptive." Given this climate of thinking, and the tendency at that time for current public expenditure generally to increase in real terms, it is no surprise that public transport systems in many countries began to receive larger subsidies. A survey of the 1970s confirmed this trend for all 24 member countries of the OECD. Nonetheless, there seems to be little reason for expecting the planning environment within which the car

---

1. A.Altshuler, *The Urban Transportation System: Politics and Policy,* MIT Press, 1979, p.37.
2. M.Hillman et al, *Transport Realities and Planning Policy,* PSI, London, 1976, p.164.
3. ibid., p.170.

industry will be operating to be significantly tougher in the coming decade. Despite resort to physical controls on urban driving (recently introduced, for instance, in Singapore and in Lagos, Nigeria) in most countries the private car seems likely to remain the pre-eminent form of transport while the planning climate will remain hostile in theory but less so in practice.

Evidence of just how substantially private car use has supplanted other road transport (such as buses) and rail comes from UK transportation statistics. In 1958, 48% of passenger kilometres were travelled in cars, 29% by bus and 17% by rail. In 1980 81% were travelled by car, only 11% by bus and only 7% by rail.

At the beginning of the 1980s the questions now most frequently asked concern not whether the industry will survive, but in what form. In particular, there are six sets of issues that are presently giving rise to fears and uncertainties, not only in the established capitals of the industry such as Detroit and Turin, but also in its newer locations such as Sao Paulo and Tunis.

The first question is of central importance for marketing. It is the question of how far the developed country markets, such as the US, Canada, Australia and West Germany, are from saturation, or that point at which sales growth becomes zero and only replacement sales, at a steady volume year after year, are found. In practice it has proved very hard to specify the point at which saturation might set in, for three reasons. First, the trend of two or multiple car ownership within a household has proved difficult to assess. Second, the demographic trend toward single-person households in advanced countries has accelerated in recent years (only some 25% of Americans, for instance, now live in two-parent, two-child households) to the point where it appears that saturation may be attained considerably later than was thought hitherto. Finally, the approach of saturation in a volume sense may be reduced in importance if the value added per car sold can continue to be increased. For in this way the manufacturers can still look forward to rising total sales revenue in years to come. The extent to which this is possible, along with the other factors mentioned here, does of course need to be examined very carefully.

The second question of importance in the industry follows from this first one: it is the growth of sales outside the traditional markets. It has long been evident that South East Asia, Latin America and some African and Middle Eastern countries were already showing rates of market growth substantially in excess of those found after the early 1970s in the west. But in all cases this growth was from a very small base. From the point of view of marketing, for instance, 2% growth in the 10,000,000 unit US market is obviously more crucial than, say, 8% growth in a 50,000 unit market such as South Korea; the difference is 200,000 units compared to 4,000. But there are many countries now approaching that stage of development where car ownership can grow explosively, and the arithmetic of compound growth, whereby, for instance, 7% per annum doubles in ten years, is very powerful. Thus the circumstances under which some of the more advanced developing countries could be the powerhouse of the car industry later in the decade is a question which needs to be addressed.

The same comments apply to the COMECON bloc. Pent-up demand in many of those countries is obviously huge, and even car prices equal to three years' average earnings have proved insufficient to choke off demand. But so long as the shift of planning priorities towards consumer durables such as cars proceeds as slowly as it has done in the recent past, there are doubts for expecting sales — or, for that matter, Western car firms' involvement — to expand very significantly.

In all portions of the world's car markets one factor which has periodically given cause for alarm has been the price of oil and its derivatives. In 1973/4 and again in 1979/80 world car production was knocked seriously off its trend growth-path with, for instance 1980's car output total of 29.36 million down 7% from the peceding year's 31.54 million. Some of the more alarmist forecasts of oil prices, such as those projecting $100/barrel oil, at 1979 prices, by the mid-1980s, have now been revised downward, and there is now a growing school forecasting stable real oil prices for much of the decade. Yet the industry does have to be prepared for further oil shocks. The nature and extent of the consequences of further oil price increases, and physical shortages, must therefore be considered in any long-run review of the industry's health.

Just as significant a development for the car industry in the 1970s as the oil shocks was the emergence, after a very short history essentially going back only to the mid-1950s, of a number of Japanese car manufacturers on world markets. In 1950 Japanese car output totalled only 31,597 units — a mere 0.3% of the world total. But by 1960 output had grown to 480,000 and by 1970 5.29 million, then equivalent to 17.8% of the world total. Exports began to appear in bulk in developing country markets in the 1960s, then became important in the non-manufacturing European markets such as Switzerland and Ireland, as well as in the west coast of the USA, and by 1981 were accounting for nearly 20% of all car exports. In 1980 Japanese car output eclipsed US output for the first time, with 7.26 million cars coming from Toyota, Nissan, Mazda, Mitsubishi, Honda, Isuzu, Subaru, Daihatsu and Suzuki.

This rapid growth of competition from Japanese producers placed many Western firms in great difficulty. In the US, it was clear that the unit cost differential which had grown up between domestic and Japanese producers was so large that, at best, it could only be eroded after five years of savage cost cutting and major reinvestment. In the meantime the size of Japanese cars suited the mix of demand far better than the big three US producers' models, particularly after 1979. The resort to a voluntary export restraint, which took effect from April 1st 1981, was virtually inevitable. In this way the US market followed a path laid down previously in many European countries.

Yet as more markets were closed to the Japanese, the entire matrix of international trade in fully assembled cars came to be threatened. And it was exactly this matrix to which the big car producers had been looking when they had planned their

4

1980s strategies of "world cars", which include the aim of cars being manufactured and assembled in various sites and shipped at will between markets to minimise costs and maximise flexibility and profit. After growing from $41 billion in 1973 to $127 billion in 1981, international trade in motor vehicles did slow down a little; but under normal circumstances would be expected to pick up later in 1982. The prospects for continued trade in cars is, then, another of the major questions which car producers must ponder in the immediate future.

Yet there are other reasons too for doubting whether the concept of the world car will be as important as was initially expected. For, quite apart from constraints on the international movement of assembled cars, another premise on which the world car was based was sufficient similarity in consumer's tastes in different markets to enable essentially similar cars to be sold across entire continents. So far there is very little evidence of this homogenization of tastes. The shares of sales in different segments of the market (such as small, intermediate, luxury) remain obstinately different in many countries. Furthermore, the very disappointing sales results obtained by the first world car, the General Motors J-car (sold in Brazil, Japan, Europe, North America, Australasia and elsewhere) serve to throw doubt upon the strategy. It may well be that only in components and certain pressings is the world car viable; and an investigation of how far even this is an economic path to follow is clearly an imperative for the industry.

This fifth issue in turn leads to the last of the six that must be addressed. Any reading of the history of the car industry shows that, in vivid comparison with others, it has always been a home-based industry whenever possible. Foreign investment has tended to be made only reluctantly, and usually at the prodding of governments anxious to protect their own firms from rising imports. As a recent history of car companies put it, their credo has always been "home sweet home country"[1]. The big question for the 1980s that follows from this is how far this preference will persist, and, consequently, whether the growing resort to protectionism, as mentioned earlier, will merely confirm the industry in its past ways or whether it will precipitate new patterns of international cooperation. The growth of joint ventures, such as those between BL and Honda, and between Alfa-Romeo and Nissan, may point to a future which involves a rather different framework of ownership and control, outside the conventional multinational corporation, than has been the norm in the post-war period. This too merits attention.

These, then, are the issues which in the early 1980s appear likely to have the greatest influence on the evolution of the world's car companies and the industry as a whole. Although taken individually virtually every car company now has its problems and faces constraints, and the industry as a whole has its difficulties, the medium-term outlook must nonetheless be judged bright. Concentration on problems should not blind outsiders to the fact that the industry will almost certainly remain a major generator of revenue and profit. In 1979, 31.05 million cars were sold worldwide. 1980

---

1. G.Maxcy, *The Multinational Motor Industry* (London: Croom Helm, 1981).

was a slip back to 28.40 million, and 1981 a further fall to 28.02 million. But as industrial output resumes its trend growth-path into the mid-1980s and households' real disposable income resumes its growth as well, there can be little doubt that a great deal of money will again be made from the business of making and selling cars.

Chapter Two

The Current Crisis in the Car Industry

Adjustments of the order outlined in Chapter 1 would be an onerous burden under any circumstances, given the intensity of price competition seen in the industry in recent years and given the vast size of the capital commitments necessary. From an industry where billion dollar losses in one company are not unknown, swings of financial fortune can be substantial and can threaten virtual elimination. Table 2.1 shows how, over the 1978-81 period, very substantial losses were incurred by many leading car firms.

TABLE 2.1

RECENT FINANCIAL PERFORMANCE OF THE CAR INDUSTRY
$ million, pretax

		$ million pretax		
		1981 sales	1981 profits	1980 profits	1979 profits
a)	**US-based firms**				
	GM	62,699	333	− 669	
	Ford	38,247	− 1,060	− 1,551	
	Chrysler	10,822	− 476	− 702	
	American Motors	2,589	− 137	− 203	
b)	**European-based firms**				
	Renault		− 175	184	240
	Peugeot Group		− 405	− 625	445
	BL		− 1,045	− 1,213	− 289
	Ford − UK		450	505	783
	Vauxhall		− 120	− 190	− 65
	Opel (after tax)		− 45	− 225	100
	BMW		70	242	340
	VW-Audi		58	1,080	1,540
	Fiat SPA (net)		76	38	
c)	**Japanese-based firms**				
	Toyota Motor (first half)	7,800	568		

Thus the financial state of many of the world's major car firms, only slowly emerging from the 1980-82 crisis, is not one which underwrites a great deal of optimism when viewing their prospects over the next few years. A brief account of how they found themselves in such a crisis is useful at this stage in helping ascertain how much of the industry's woes might be expected to correct themselves as time passes, and how much can be expected to persist.

The fundamental conditions facing virtually all business in the early 1980s (excluding, to some degree, Japan and parts of the oil industry) are well known. One of the most severe post-war recessions has plagued the European economy, while the US has, technically, undergone not one but two recessions, in mid-1980 and 1982. The oil crisis of 1979 found most Western governments with their own spending still over-expanded from the last oil crisis, of 1973-4, and consequently much less able than before to lean into the wind and add to private demand through higher levels of public expenditure. Another factor at work after late 1979 was the initiation of a new and tougher monetary policy in the USA, the main consequence of which was a much great volatility in US interest-rates. The tighter stance of the US monetary authorities made an immediate impact on the US dollar, which gained ground against the European currencies to an unanticipated extent during the following two years. Forcing up the domestic currency cost of imported oil (which is, of course, priced in dollars) this faced European countries with, in effect, a third oil shock. It also forced many European governments into a recession-inducing round of interest-rate increases, in an attempt to defend their own currencies, as far as possible, against further depreciation against the dollar.

For the car industry the consequences of this were immediately apparent: interest-rates which rose in a recession (the reverse of the normal pattern) deterred owners buying on credit while encouraging a higher proportion of earnings to be put into savings rather than into consumption. Meanwhile those same interest-rate increases were affecting employment and output, not only in the two most interest-sensitive sectors of cars and housing, but eventually throughout much of the economy at large. Observing rising unemployment and squeezed real disposable income, as mortgage payments rose in sympathy with higher international interest-rates, consumers simply slowed down the rate at which they replaced their cars. The life of cars, and other consumer durables, was extended — a reaction open to consumers at all times, but one which can have a particularly savage impact upon car producers in a recession.

As if these factors were not enough to worry the manufacturers, a further depressing factor was affecting new car sales: the very rapid rise in car prices seen in the later years of the 1970s. After a prolonged period in which the price of cars (relative to income) had been falling, their real price began to pick up again quite sharply in the late 1970s. The companies in the US tended to blame this on the costly effects of the regulations imposed by Washington on safety, on emissions rules and other factors.

As table 2.2 shows, the relationship between the cost of buying and running a car, and average take home pay, certainly changed for the worse after 1977 — a change which was quite closely reflected in the US industry's sales performance. Moreover, the 1970s had, in real terms, not delivered the accustomed increase in living standards that Americans had become used to since 1945. The Census Bureau announced early in 1982 that "real family income was virtually unchanged from 1970 to 1980 . . . in terms of buying power, families are little different today than they were in 1970"[1].

Table 2.2

AUTO PURCHASING POWER IN THE US

	(1) Index of Auto costs	(2) Average Take-home pay $	(3) (2) ÷ (1) $	(4) Auto sales (mill.)
1967	.827	4,725	5,713	8.3
1968	.890	4,955	5,567	9.7
1969	.974	5,199	5,338	9.6
1970	1.030	5,455	5,296	8.4
1971	1.020	5,846	5,731	10.2
1972	1.010	6,327	6,264	10.9
1973	1.059	6,624	6,255	11.4
1974	1.213	7,000	5,771	8.9
1975	1.337	7,574	5,665	8.6
1976	1.438	8,105	5,636	10.1
1977	1.519	8,836	5,817	11.2
1978	1.621	9,397	5,797	11.3
1979	1.985	9,256	4,663	10.7
1980	2.535	9,819	3,873	9.0
1981	3.016	11,310	3,750	8.5

Sources: Data Resources, US Department of Labor

Source: "The Auto Industry: Posed for a Rebound", *Value Line,* 5:3:82.

1. "Inflation wiped out gains in earnings in 1970s". *New York Times,* 25:4:82.

In Europe, a rather different story pertained, with a marked slowing in the rate of productivity growth shortening the link between higher wages and higher prices. Chart 1 shows how, as a percentage of household expenditure, transport outlays had been growing rapidly for all European consumers for much of the post-war period. It seems likely, in retrospect, that the sharp rise in petrol and purchase prices seen after 1979 had an effect upon consumers' perceptions of the cost of buying and running a new car. As a result they stayed out of the car showrooms in droves. (However, an exception to this should be noted in the case of Italy. There the real price of cars eased appreciably during 1980 and 1981, helping sustain an unexpectedly buoyant period of car sales despite a seriously deteriorating economic picture.)

The natural consequence of this increased real cost was less frequent car replacement and thus diminished fresh demand. The median age of cars in the USA increased accordingly, from 4.9 years in 1970 to 5.4 years in 1975 and 6.0 years in early 1982[1].

Related to this difficulty was the increasingly capricious behaviour of consumers in their car purchasing. The 1973 oil price increases had, of course, been expected to switch car buyers' preferences very strongly towards smaller, more fuel-efficient models. Yet the pattern of car buying during the post-1973 period was not quite so clearcut, and the car firms experienced the greatest difficulty in correctly identifying the factors driving changes in tastes. Given the long lead times which characterize the business, with four years at least needed from conceiving a model to having the tested cars in dealers' showrooms, this made for an extremely volatile planning environment. Cars can in practice be altered considerably during this design and prototype stage: as a study of the Ford Fiesta's development put it, "the development of a new car is an infinite succession of compromises, a process of evolving priorities"[2]. But this adds to costs and it adds to the problems of those marketing staffs whose job it is to fit in the new model alongside those which the company already produces. Too big an alteration in the car's design may result in its pulling away sales from other models made by the same firm; at the same time, too individual a design may fracture the image which the firm is attempting to establish through the overall appearance and characteristics of its products.

An illustration of the reactions of consumers to the oil price rises can be seen in table 2.3, and Chart 2, which show the shares of the US car market accounted for by the various segments. Demand for small cars (that is, lighter and smaller than the conventional 'full sized' American saloon cars) had first appeared in the late 1950s, only to be dealt with by US firms' own products (and, to some extent, tied imports from their European subsidiaries). Again in the second half of the 1960s, led chiefly by VW, demand for small cars grew once more. After 1973, while there was a continuing strong interest in such cars, all experience thereafter showed that the full-sized car was to be preferred, whenever possible, by the US consumer. As was often to be

---

1. "Driven to hold onto old cars". *Newsday*, 25:4:82.
2. E. Seidler, *Let's Call It Fiesta* (Lausanne, Edita, 1976).

CHART 1

PRIVATE TRANSPORT EXPENDITURE AS A PERCENTAGE OF TOTAL HOUSEHOLD CONSUMPTION

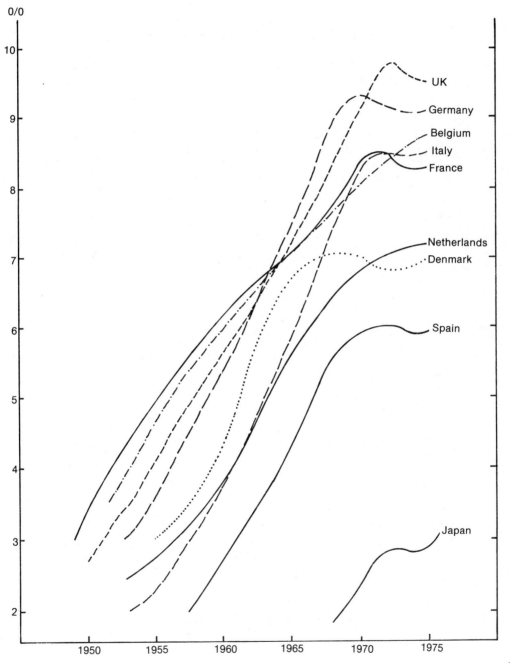

pointed out subsequently, in January 1979 — a month before the fall of the Shah of Iran — there were 850,000 unsold high-economy Japanese cars at American docksides. Nobody wanted them.

Table 2.3

SHARES OF CARS BY SIZE CATEGORY, 1972-1982, in USA, % OF MARKET

Year	Full sized cars, % (luxury plus standard)	Small cars % (compact plus sub-compact)
1972	40.9	21.3
1973	37.3	23.3
1974	28.5	26.6
1975	24.3	29.1
1976	24.5	24.9
1977	26.3	26.6
1978	25.1	28.7
1979	23.2	26.6
1980	18.1	42.0
1981	16.2	42.5
1982[a]	17.4	42.5

[a] 1st four months
Source: "Oil glut worries automakers", *Detroit Free Press,* 3:5:82.

Reactions did, however, change rather more suddenly after the 1979 oil shock. Least well prepared for this was the US division of Ford Motor Company, which, partly from an examination of figures such as those in Table 2.3 and Chart 2 decided that for the next five years at least it should return to stressing the conventional full-sized car. Its sales fell drastically and in 1980 Ford's share of the US market tumbled to only 15.9% after 20.1% in 1979. Its 1981 share, at 16.2%, was little better. With GM, Chrysler, American Motors and VW of America barely changed, imports rose from 22% of sales in 1979 to 27% in both 1980 and 1981. By comparison, the General Motors X-car, available from mid-1978, was exactly what was desired in the oil-short period that was to follow.

However, yet another problem presented itself after 1979. Having struggled to invest in entirely new car product lines, in anticipation this time of a permanent shift in

CHART 2

US NEW-CAR SALES, SHARES BY MARKET CLASS, SINCE 1974

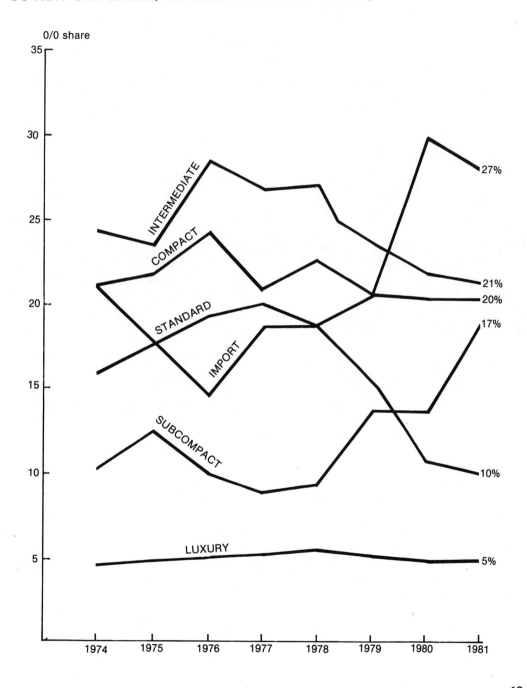

real oil prices, the firms found that consumers were very reluctant to pay the higher prices needed by the companies to recoup their investments. Consumers who had obtained full-sized saloons in 1974 for $3,000 were now faced with $9,999 prices on considerably smaller cars — many of which, moreover, were initially plagued with quality defects. This problem, which in US dealership circles was known as 'sticker shock', had far from disappeared even by mid-1982, despite prolonged rebate, interest-rate subsidy and price-cutting exercises mounted by the manufacturers[1]. What made this period even more awkward for producers was the realization that excess capacity throughout the world's oil refining industry coupled with a levelling-out in the real price of oil, was reversing petrol prices at the retail level. During 1982 gasoline was obtainable in some parts of the USA for just under $1 per gallon again, and at that price the trade-off between enhanced fuel efficiency and a much higher initial price told in favour of using full-sized rather than the new fuel-efficient models. Once again, there were backlogs of unsold cars — but this time they were economy models.

Perhaps the clearest indication of this apparently perverse consumer behaviour was the sales reception of the GM J-car, which was tooled at a cost of nearly $5 billion to sell all over the world to economy-conscious drivers. Introduced in May 1981 the cars attained less than half the 410,000 volume of sales expected in the USA in their first eleven months[2]. More important than the failure of that model itself, though, is that its dismal reception has been taken by the car firms as further evidence of their having misread consumer tastes and engineering needs. A US car analyst reportedly said of the cars' poor start that it has made "GM sceptical about its ability to design and build a small car here".

Another factor likely to have been at work in 1980-82 was the differential impact of unemployment on US car buyers. The worst-hit by unemployment were, as in any recession, disproportionately the unskilled and the lower-paid, who would tend to buy less expensive cars. In contrast the better-off households experienced no major loss of earnings and in consequence sales of full-sized cars continued relatively strong. In the first five months of model year 1982, for instance, full-sized cars took 18.5% of the market, as against 16.8% in the preceding year[3].

This hesitation, on the part of consumers, regarding the attractions of full-sized cars, even prompted the president of Chrysler to call for a 25 cents per gallon excise tax to promote sales of smaller cars. Lee Iococoa of Chrysler was also trying, for much of 1982, to have a $1,500 tax credit awarded to those individuals who bought cars giving better than 25 m.p.g. Meanwhile, in the colourful prose of the *New York Times,* "the big car, that smooth-riding, chrome bedecked land yacht that once seemed part of the American birthright, is making a modest comeback on the nation's highways after apparently being doomed to extinction by high gasoline prices".

---

1 "US car sales tumble despite promotions". *The Times,* 7:4:82.
2 "GM's J-car campaign hits snags". *Herald Tribune,* 27:4:82.
3 "Shift back to big cars worries auto makers". *New York Times,* 21:2:82.

14

CHART 3

US AUTOMOBILE FUEL ECONOMY

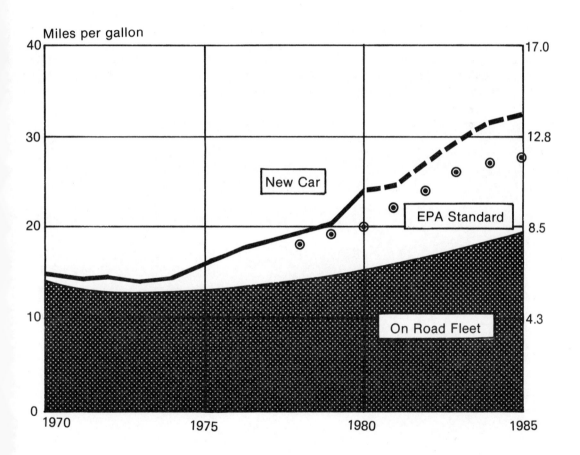

As stated at the beginning of this chapter, then, the evidence at mid-1982 strongly suggested that the large US-based car firms faced two substantial areas of difficulty. Even assuming that car demand in the US built up later in 1982 and through 1983 to approach again its levels of 1979, two facts have changed for the industry. First, there has been a substantial loss of cash reserves and a large build-up of debt during the past three years. And second, the degree of uncertainty surrounding the entire product planning philosophy of the firms — to move as fast as possible, right across the product range, towards much more fuel-efficient cars — has been called into question. Of course, there is a constraint to the latter decision in the form of US Federal fuel-efficiency regulations, as shown in Chart 3. But the extent to which the firms intend to exceed these minima could be reconsidered and indeed the rigour of the minima themselves could presumably be altered in the face of determined lobbying by the car firms' representatives, under favourable circumstances.

These, then, are the chief difficulties which face the firms which are intending to pursue the path of the world car, to a greater or lesser extent. The attractions and pitfalls of that path are examined in some depth in Chapter 7.

Chapter Three

The Oil Scare and its Consequences

The question of oil price and availability is, clearly, of paramount importance for the car industry. Although, as past experience has demonstrated, it seems unlikely that even a succession of oil price increases similar to those witnessed in the 1970s would entirely choke off demand for new cars, there is no doubt that such an eventuality would massively affect the pattern of demand growth and the type of car (or the mix of demand) sought by consumers. It is useful, therefore, to examine briefly the changes brought about in the industry in the 1970s due to the oil price rises, and the extent of the industry's preparedness for a repetition of these shocks.

During the 1950s and 1960s an assured supply of oil at falling real prices appeared to be a reasonable assumption to make in all planning, but with the 1971 oil price revisions and the dramatic increases and the embargo of 1973 this parameter became a variable. Again in 1979 and 1980, after a period of relative quiet on the international oil market, physical oil supply was disturbed and prices again rocketed. This time the impact of the price rises was considerably more profound on the economics and forecasting professions and, rather than assuming a return to the relative lull of the mid-1970s scenarios increasingly pointed to greater and greater disruption. Forecasting continued political upheaval in the Middle East, with coups and revolutions in emulation of that which toppled the Shah of Iran, analysts expected the price of a barrel of oil to rise from its end-1979 value of $18 to $60 or even $100, in constant prices, by the second half of the 1980s. For the car industry the consequences were, clearly, forecast to be particularly severe. The volume of sales was expected to collapse from its long-term growth trend. The markets in the developing world were expected to be aborted straight away, given the balance of payments constraints that would henceforth face all oil-importing developing countries. Furthermore, the rapid growth switch in demand expected, towards small and ultra-economy models, appeared to threaten the financial wellbeing of the established US producers. For not only would the task of retooling the entire range of cars be prohibitively expensive, but in the process the most lucrative slice of the market — the full-sized sedan — was expected to disappear. As if this were not enough, an interim period during the switchover of capacity would send US (and to a lesser extent European) purchasers into the arms of Japanese producers, whose capacity for high-quality fuel-efficient models was growing all the time.

In their widely-read study, *Running on Empty: The Future of the Automobile in an Oil-Short World*[1], Lester Brown and his collaborators took the view that while the rise in the oil price "does not necessarily mean that the end of the automobile age is in

---

1 Published by W.W.Norton, 1979.

sight, it does suggest that things will never be quite the same. These shocks do not signal the demise of the automobile but they do suggest a marked slowdown in the "automobilization" of the world". Yet only four years after this study was published, perceptions about fuels scarcity have changed greatly and there is again renewed confidence about the so-called automobilization of the world. Even the third world, which, OPEC members apart, most observers expected never to reach the automobile age in a high-cost energy world, are already seeing sales booming again. Indeed, in 1981 car sales among the five ASEAN countries (Malaysia, Indonesia, Thailand, Singapore and the Philippines) grew by 17% to 502,000 units. In 1982 they are expected to have grown by another 5% to 528,000 units. The scope for optimism over these countries' prospects was further increased during 1982 as the price of both spot and contract barrels of oil fell, easing the current account deficits of the oil-importing developing countries.

In the event, then, many fears proved to be grossly exaggerated. In particular, the mechanisms whereby markets clear were underestimated. The collapse of demand for oil at the new higher prices was not fully expected; nor was the search for new sources of supply; nor was the coming onstream of three significant non-OPEC oil exporters, Norway, the UK and Mexico.

The erosion of the level of real oil prices set in 1980, during the following two years, has led a number of forecasters to rethink drastically their energy outlooks for the 1980s. In 1982 it was commonplace to find projections of world oil demand being revised downward substantially, and with them, oil price trajectories. Not only were a number of well-known forecasting services now forecasting flat oil prices for much of the next decade; but several were even pointing to prices staying below $30 (or, in a few cases, below $20) for the decade.

Whatever the outcome, what matters for the car industry in the 1980s is the realization that the oil price outlook is highly uncertain. What also matters is that experiences since 1973, and, more particularly, since 1979, show how volumes of sales and the type of car most demanded can respond. The task for the industry is therefore to maximise its ability to respond flexibly to future developments, while bearing in mind that the status quo, i.e. an oil price of about $32/barrel in real terms, also has a reasonable probability of persisting.

This is all very well, but the fact facing volume planners in the car industry is that flexibility costs money. It means having spare capacity ready to boost production of small models at short notice; it also means having sufficient capacity to cope with the relatively price-resistant buyer of middle-sized cars who, as has been seen, tends to return to the marketplace after any oil price rises. In a decade which is beginning with high interest-rates (and many forecasters believe these will persist well into the mid-1980s) this type of excess capacity is going to be extremely costly to build and maintain. Arguing from this point, certain forecasters have predicted that only the largest firms, with the ability to cope with such financing strains, will be able to survive. But there are grounds for doubting this, as Chapter 7 will show. In the mean-

18

time, however, the point which should not be overlooked is that the post-1973 oil market is undeniably more prone to interruption than before. Since virtually the only weapon the car companies have to defend themselves with in the face of this uncertainty is (costly) spare capacity, there is further ground for short-term pessimism about the financial health of the western car firms.

Chapter 4

The International Car Industry in the 1970s

I.   The eclipse of European exports

A major characteristic of international trade flows in the car industry since the 1960s has been the eclipse of the European and North American firms' shares in world trade. Japan has grown very quickly to become the indisputable major source of car exports to the world market. The USA had never been a particularly significant car exporter, with US firms' exports peaking at only 181,000 units (or 2.3% of US domestic car production) in 1964. In that year, the UK, Italy, France and Germany each exported more cars than the US, and even West German exports of second-hand cars were equivalent to nearly half of the American volume. The European producing countries, by contrast, had long been recognised as the primary sources of traded cars, and there can be little doubt that the manufacturers involved saw continued export growth as a crucial part of their long-term evolution.

TABLE 4.1

EUROPEAN CAR EXPORTS BY COUNTRY OF ORIGIN:
Year of Highest Exports and 1980 Level of Exports

Country	Year of highest exports	(Volume)	1980 export volume
UK	1969	771,600	359,145
France	1979	1,535,000	1,373,000
West Germany	1979	2,283,000	2,108,000
Italy	1976	696,400	511,200
Sweden	1971	212,480	154,500

Source: SMMT (1982)

During the 1970s, however, several of the main exporting countries (the UK, France, West Germany, Italy and Sweden) saw their export volumes plateau and then fall back. As table 4.1 shows, the UK and Sweden were the first to see their firms' exports peak, in 1964 and 1971 respectively. By 1980 British firms' exports stood at less than half their peak level of 771,600 cars, while Swedish firms' exports slipped from 1971 to a low-point of 131,000 in 1977 before picking up again slightly. Italian firms' exports, after peaking in 1976, have been in fairly steady decline, with the 1980 volume of 511,200 cars back down to the level previously achieved in 1967. French and West German export trends do not fully accord with this pattern, with only slight slippage after 1979, and prior steady growth.

The question which the French and German experience raises is, clearly, that of cyclical reversal versus trend. In other words, to what extent can the fall in export volumes witnessed in those two countries after 1979 be reversed in the mid-1980s, or how far is it irreversible? And if it is likely to prove irreversible, will the decline follow the patterns exhibited by the UK, Italy and Sweden, and if so why? In particular, in view of the publicity given to recent forecasts of Europe as a whole becoming a net car importer by the mid-1980s, one needs to examine the issue of how European-based firms are going to deal with this prospect of a serious reversal of their past experience.

TABLE 4.2

JAPANESE FIRMS' SHARE IN WORLD EXPORTS OF CARS, BY VOLUME, 1957-1980, AND VOLUME OF EXPORTS

Year	%	number of exports (thousands)
1957	0.03	0.4
1967	6.5	224
1970	13.7	726
1973	22.3	1,451
1976	34.5	2,539
1980	45.6	3,947
1981	n/a	3,950

Source: calculated from SMMT, (1982).

There are three issues which have to be addressed in this connection. The first is the subject of Japanese exports. As table 4.2 makes clear, there is no doubting that the overwhelming gainers in world trade markets in the 1970s have been the Japanese-based firms. From taking well under 1% of world exports (defined here as exports of the big eight countries: the UK, France, West Germany, Italy, Sweden, Japan, Canada and the USA) in 1957 and 6.5% in 1967, the Japanese share has grown very substantially. It exceeded 13% in 1970 and by 1980 reached nearly 46%.

Although total trade in cars was growing throughout the period, the enormous growth of the Japanese market share was such that, as just illustrated, many European firms' absolute export volumes were pushed downwards.

The second issue is how far the fall in European firms' share in world trade reflects other factors, such as a less aggressive assembly programme in the fast-growing markets of certain developing countries, and their consequent virtual exclusion from important sales areas. The final issue is how far, in contrast to the proposition just stated, the fall in European exports reflects not so much a crisis as a maturing of the European firms. This interpretation would seek to establish that through greater use of international plant locations and transfers of components (as opposed to fully-assembled cars) the export figures are merely revealing steady progress towards one or other of the world car concepts previously alluded to.

TABLE 4.3

VALUE OF IMPORTS OF CARS BY SOURCE COUNTRIES, BY VALUE, 1973-1980, $ billion

| Year | World | Value of imports to: | | | | |
		N.America	W.Europe	Japan	OPEC	non-OPEC ldcs[1]
1973	41	15	16	.2	2	4
1978	99	32	39	.5	9	11
1979	115	35	49	.7	9	12
1980	127	37	55	.6	— 29 —	

1. Less Developed Countries

Examination of the matrix of international trade in cars, by value, prepared annually by GATT allows one to settle the former question quite unambiguously. There is no doubt that it is in Europe that the relative importance of Japanese-built cars within total car imports has grown fastest. Tables 4.3 and 4.4 show the values of imports and exports of cars by area, from 1973 to 1980, expressed in current dollar terms. Calculated from GATT figures, these tables indicate how the Japanese share of world exports has grown from 5% to 27% between 1973 and 1980, while the country's importance as a car importer has remained trivial at under 1% of world imports. In absolute terms, the biggest increase in imports has occurred in Western Europe, where the value of car imports has risen from $16 billion in 1973 to $55 billion in 1980. (In percentage terms, by contrast, the developing countries, taken together, have seen the fastest growth, with $6 billion-worth of car imports in 1973 transformed to $29 billion-worth by 1980.) At the same time as this has happened, European firms'

23

TABLE 4.4

VALUE OF WORLD EXPORTS OF CARS, BY AREA, BY VALUE, 1973-1980, $ billion

Year	World	N.America	W.Europe	Japan	OPEC	non-OPEC ldcs
1973	41	11	22	2	0	0
1978	99	23	51	19	0	.5
1979	115	24	63	21	0	.6
1980	127	27	55	27	0	n.a.

TABLE 4.5

JAPANESE FIRMS' SHARE IN IMPORTS, BY AREA, %, 1973-1980

Year	World	N.America	W.Europe	Japan	OPEC	non-OPEC ldcs
1973	12	17	5	—	4	16
1978	19	28	8	—	14	16
1979	18	21	7	—	11	15
1980	21	33	16	—	— 32 —	

TABLE 4.6

EUROPEAN FIRMS' SHARE IN IMPORTS, BY AREA, %, 1973-1980

Year	World	N.America	W.Europe	Japan	OPEC	non-OPEC ldcs
1973	53	25	—	50	55	47
1978	51	19	—	65	43	41
1979	55	19	—	61	43	43
1980	58	21	—	67	— 47 —	

importance as exporters to the rest of the world has slipped back, with European firms' sales abroad accounting for 54% of world imports by value in 1973 but only 43% in 1980. It is ironic to note that European firms also accounted for approximately two-thirds of Japanese car imports in 1980 (see table 4.6). But since the total value of Japanese car imports in that year was a mere $600 million, this success counted for very little.

Some statistical points should be noted here: large disparities in data showing the importance of countries as car exporters or importers frequently occur. These can be traced to two causes. First, volume and value terms diverge considerably. In 1980, for instance, Japan accounted for 28% of industrial countries' exports of motor vehicles and parts (by value) but for 41% of exports by volume. The tendency for Japanese cars to cost less than other firms' cars thus tends to underrepresent the former's importance in trade. As the 1981 GATT review observed, "one notes that the average value of a Japanese vehicle is less than one-half of its US or German equivalent. This is largely due to the different product mix which also explains that although Japan exported roughly as many automobiles as the EEC, the value of the EEC's exports of finished automobiles exceeded that of Japan by 80% in 1980"[1]. Second, expressing all car exports in current US dollar terms also distorts value terms. There has been considerable volatility in the movement of the US dollar against the European currencies, and also the Japanese yen, in the second half of the 1970s (and the early 1980s), and this makes straightforward value comparisons still more hazardous. For instance, between October 1979 and March 1980 the yen depreciated by 40% against the DM, 33% against the French franc and by 45% against sterling.

II   The growth of Japanese exports

The growth of Japanese car exports in the 1970s owes a considerable amount to government intervention and careful planning over the post-war period. Although the main US-based firms had an interest in Japanese plants as early as 1924, the 35% tariff on foreign-built cars was not sufficient to deter imports on any significant scale, and most of the market was provided from US plants. In 1936 foreign companies began to be squeezed out of Japan's car industry, however, and in 1938 were expelled. In an effort to assist the build-up of army supplies, indigenous Japanese firms were established during the 1930s. After the devastation of the war it fell again to the government, aided by the powerful trade and industry ministry MITI, to rebuild the industry, and this objective was pursued so aggressively and successfully that by 1967 Japan became the world's second biggest car producing country. Shortly after that date, and apparently in contradiction to the wishes of MITI, a number of Japanese companies established links with US majors (Mitsubishi with Chrysler, Toyo Kogyo with Ford and Isuzu with GM). Nevertheless the prime objective of MITI, to push through sufficient mergers to have consolidated and efficient firms poised to take advantage of the eventual liberalization of the Japanese market to foreign imports,

---

1. GATT, *International Trade 1980/81*, (GATT, Geneva, 1981), p.85.

had been achieved. To quote a recent survey, "Japanese firms are the unique independent newcomers since world war II to the select ranks of the western world's major motor car producers"[1].

TABLE 4.7

SHARE OF JAPANESE EXPORTS IN REGISTRATIONS, 1968-1979, BY IMPORTING COUNTRY IN EUROPE

Country	1966	1970	1975	1979	1981
Belgium	0.3	4.9	16.5	18.0	28%
France	0	0.2	1.6	2.2	2%
Germany	0	0.1	1.7	5.6	10%
Italy	0	0	0.1	0.1	—
Netherlands	0.6	3.2	15.5	19.5	26%
UK	0.1	0.4	9.0	10.8	10%
Denmark	0.5	3.4	14.7	18.1	28%
Ireland	0	0	8.9	25.2	30%
Austria	0	0.9	5.4	12.4	23%
Switzerland	0.1	5.6	8.4	16.0	26%
Portugal	0	10.7	11.8	7.8	11%
Finland	14.4	18.3	20.8	23.9	26%
Norway	1.9	11.4	28.4	24.2	36%
Sweden	0.2	0.7	6.5	10.0	14%

The initial concentration of the Japanese producers, when exporting, lay in the relatively close and fast-expanding south east Asian markets, which very quickly they came to dominate. By 1982 Asia (other than Japan itself) was taking 10% of the total Japanese car exports, with a volume of 594,000 units. Their dominance in Indonesia (a market of 225,000 units in 1982) and Malaysia (130,000 units) was nearly complete, at more than 80%, by the same year. This initial strategy was well suited due to the early Japanese concentration on small and relatively inexpensive models, of the sort that would be of obvious appeal to the emergent middle classes of the ASEAN states.

Towards the late 1960s, however, the US too became an increasingly important

1. G.Shepherd, "The Japanese Challenge to Western Europe's new crisis Industries", *The World Economy,* 1981.

market for Japanese firms. Seeing the continued success of VW sales in the US (which peaked at nearly 600,000 units in 1968 and 1970) the Japanese firms were able to confirm the existence of a market for low-priced compact models, and by 1973 Toyota and Datsun were together selling 530,000 units annually. 1979 and 1980 saw particularly strong growth of Japanese sales in the US market.

A similar story unfolded in Europe. Initially, the Japanese exporters concentrated on the markets without indigenous producers: Norway, Finland and Switzerland were among the first markets to witness rising Japanese penetration. Overall the Japanese share of the EEC market (defined to include the UK throughout) rose from 0.1% in 1960 to 0.6% in 1970 and then to 4.7% by 1975. Thereafter the Japanese share grew steadily, to 7.3% by 1979. From 233,000 units in 1973, Japanese sales grew to 786,000 in 1979. The growth of Japanese net exports to Europe in value terms has been such that a net deficit, on the part of Europe, of $346 million in 1973 grew to $2.24 billion by 1979. (See table 4.7.)

It should be pointed out that what is recorded here is by no means unique to that industry. Across a wide range of industries, Japanese exports have grown exceptionally rapidly since the 1950s. Motorcycles, ships, electronic consumer goods, cameras, and, more recently, machine tools, are only a few of the industries which have been affected in this way. What each of these industries tends to have in common is an early identification by the Japanese planning agencies of a niche towards which they would strive, and a consolidation of firms whenever necessary. It would appear that, as far as cars are concerned, Japan's share of world trade has merely followed the path illuminated by other industries.

Chapter Five

The COMECON Market: Frustrated Demand to Continue

At first glance the prospects of very rapid growth for car sales in the eastern bloc would appear excellent. Pent-up demand is clearly there. Personal savings are substantial, with even a worker on average earnings in the USSR unable to find enough consumer goods to absorb fully his or her income. The desire for motorization is also clearly there — people save and *manoeuver* for years to be able to own a car, even though conditions for motorists are terrible. (There are, for example, barely half a dozen petrol stations, open to the general public in the whole of Moscow; 8 million people and 250,000 cars must share these facilities.) But will these demands be satisfied in the 1980s? And if so, to what extent might western firms be able to benefit from the opportunities which arise from this? This chapter examines the prospects.

TABLE 5.1

CAR PRODUCTION, SELECTED EASTERN EUROPEAN COUNTRIES
(thousand units)

	USSR	Czech.	E.Germany	Poland	Yugoslavia	Romania
1975	1,201	175	159	173	183	53
1976	1,239	179	164	229	193	60
1977	1,280	159	167	295	231	70
1978	1,312	160	171	326	252	72
1979	1,314	172	180	363	285	74
1980	1,300	184	180	351	255	75
1981	1,400	180	175	320	n/a	n/a

Source: 1977-78 — Ford of Europe
1981 — estimates only

It is not widely realised that the USSR was a major vehicle producer in the inter-war period. Output of vehicles reached 211,100 in 1938, equivalent to 5.3% of world output. That volume placed the USSR fifth behind the USA (with 2.51 million units), the UK (444,000), Germany (342,000) and France (227,000) and well ahead of Canada (166,000) or Italy (71,000). Elsewhere in what is now Eastern Europe, Czechoslovakia produced 13,000 units, Hungary 790 and Poland 2,900. Output built up quite rapidly after the war, however, as shown in Table 5.1. The single biggest source is clearly the USSR, with the Togliatti plant, on the Volga, alone producing some 660,000 cars annually. What accounts for some of the difference between Soviet output and output elsewhere in Eastern Europe is greater exports. In the mid-1970s typically 5% of Soviet car output was exported, and this volume gave the USSR approximately a two-thirds share in all Eastern European car exports to Western Europe. Although these exports together represented only between 1% and 1.5% of the European market, fears over the involvement of certain Western firms in expansion plans in Eastern Europe grew towards the late 1970s. Table 5.2 shows how imports from each country source grew, and how the Soviet dominance in the group was maintained. The final line in the table also shows how exports took a steadily rising proportion of total output during the 1970s.

TABLE 5.2

SALES OF EASTERN EUROPEAN CARS IN WESTERN EUROPE, 1974-1981, (thousand units)

Country of origin	1974	1975	1976	1977	1978	1979	1980	1981
USSR	34.8	60.1	72.2	76.9	87.2	101.8	105.0	141.0
Czechoslovakia	19.7	26.9	24.4	25.6	23.8	21.5		
E.Germany	4.2	3.8	4.1	3.8	3.7	2.5		
Yugoslovia	3.8	5.0	4.6	3.2	3.1	4.8		
Poland	4.8	8.8	11.7	16.0	24.6	23.1		
Total:	67.3	104.6	117.0	125.5	142.4	153.7		
Share of sales in Western Europe (%)	0.8	1.3	1.2	1.3	1.4	1.5		
E.European exports as a % of output:	3.7	5.4	5.7	5.7	6.2	6.6		

Source: Ford

The important question arising from these figures concerns the extent to which Eastern European output is increasingly bound for Western markets. Will cars, in other words, follow the pattern laid down by other items such as certain types of bulk petrochemicals, whereby a Western firm sells consultancy work and capital equipment to the USSR, obtains payment in cash and in kind, after which the other Western firms in the same industry have to fend off the output sent to the West from the new Eastern plant to defray the capital charges? This is a fear which is increasingly widespread in the West, and one for which there does appear to be a substantial body of evidence. First, there is quite evidently the need of the Eastern bloc in general to earn more hard currency. 1981 and 1982 saw substantial sales of gold by the USSR (an estimated 700 tons, equal to the period's entire production) helping to depress the price, as wheat imports from the USA had to be paid for and as oil earnings diminished during the worldwide slack oil market. Although oil and gold together have in recent years been accounting for around half of the USSR's hard currency earnings, these are uncertain sources of convertible income, and the more semi-processed and manufactured goods the Soviets can begin exporting, the more diversified and secure their foreign earnings will become. There is an additional point that all modern experience shows that exposure to international trade helps sharpen quality and efficiency for domestic sales too, and planners and officials have in recent years been trying to purge Soviet manufacturing plants of their indifferent cost control and poor quality reputation.

Evidence of the Eastern European interest in growing car exports comes from more direct sources too — from the Western firms involved in the deals and from the trade press. Table 5.3 reproduces the latest available estimates of car plant expansions, suggesting that by the mid-1980s a further 1.5 million annual units of output might have been added to capacity. In view of the rising share of exports in total output, it is reasonable to expect some further increment to exports from this planned expansion, but estimates of the proportion vary considerably. A number of European car firms believe that East European sales could be accounting for as much as 7% of the West European market by 1985. From relatively small levels (1.3% in 1975 and 1.5% in 1979, for examle) COMECON-sourced cars are now seen as a serious source of further foreign competition, second only to Japanese firms' exports. In May 1982 Lada announced plans to take its Western penetration further still, with 5,000 Niva jeep-cars to be built annually at a plant in Canada. Initially, bodies, engines and transmissions will all be imported from the USSR.

What basis is there for such alarmist projections? Industry spokesmen tend sometimes to overlook that to produce a car is one thing, to sell it quite another. For the characteristics of the European car market by the mid-1980s are in fact unlikely to be such as to welcome Eastern European models unreservedly. First, the share of small cars (and these models will be small in body size and engine capacity, for only in that way will there be any spillover into economies of scale for production for home sales, which have to be of economical cars) is not particularly large in some European countries. Italy, Spain and France are those with the most important small car markets; in Germany, the UK and the Scandinavian markets the bulk of the market is accounted for by below-medium sized cars and larger. And it is Italy, Spain and France which historically have tended to keep the tightest rein on imported cars.

TABLE 5.3

EASTERN EUROPEAN CAR PRODUCTION EXPANSION PLANS

Model Year	Country	Involving	European Assistance	Production Volumes 1978 (000)	Production Volumes 1985* (000)
1980 ½	Yugoslavia	Zastava 102	Fiat	51	120
	Romania	Dacia Replacement	Renault	73	110
1981	USSR	Lada Facelift	—	740	740
1981	Yugoslavia	Assembly Plant	Opel	—	8
1981-82	Romania	LN Replacement	PSA	—	175
1981 ½-2	East Germany/ Yugoslavia	Wartburg Replacement	PSA	115	250
1982	USSR	Zaphorozet Replacement	Porsche	120	300
1982	Yugoslavia	305, 504, 604 Assembly	PSA	—	25
1983	East Germany/ Czechoslovakia	Estelle Replacement	—	173	200
1983/4	USSR	Moskvich Replacement	VW	400	500
1984/5	East Germany/ Czechoslovakia	Trabant Replacement	PSA	56	340
By 1985	Poland	Polski 126 Replacement	Fiat	188	400
By 1985	Yugoslavia	Additional Renault models	Renault	34	150
Other	Capacity Expansions			37	170
	Existing Models			320	320
	Total Car Production			2,307	3,808

*Projected potential production

Source: Ford of Europe, press release, Sept. 1980.

Second, these cars will be sold initially on price competitiveness, given that design, luxury, quality control and handling will all be either unknown factors or factors which tell against them given previous experience in the West. Already, it is clear that Soviet, Polish and similar imports are sold at well below the prices obtained in the countries of their manufacture. But the question of the importance of the market for relatively unattractively designed cars at very low prices is by no means obvious. Consumers who require very inexpensive car transportation can buy second-hand cars. At least that way they have some idea of the resale value their cars are likely to commend. Families which require a second household car might be interested — but there already exists a substantial choice of such cars which at mid-1982 prices cost less than £3,500 in the UK. At that time, retail prices of Soviet-built Lada cars, for instance, ranged from £2,499 to £3,300 and Zastava Yugo cars, built in Yugoslavia, and derived from the Fiat 128, cost between £2,699 and £3,362. The Czech-built Skoda 1055 cost £2,149. The Skoda apart, there are a number of well-regarded models from established producers, such as the Citroen 2CV6, at £2,475, the Datsun Cherry L at £2,945, the Ford Fiesta Popular, at £3,255 and others such as the Mini Metro, Citroen Visa, Vauxhall Chevette and Fiat Strada. Moreover, these comparisons are against UK retail prices — which are by far the highest of any European market. Elsewhere in Western Europe, the price differential will be correspondingly less, even after, as is bound to be the case, the East European firms have adjusted their quoted prices to reflect the overall level of prices. Given their other attributes, then, it may be reasonable to expect Eastern European models to be of interest to Western purchasers only at prices, say, 15%-20% at least below the price of equivalent Western cars.

In addition, it is probable that a portion of the Eastern European-built cars offered for sale in Western Europe will in any case be sold under the aegis of Western companies. Fiat's Zero, to be built in Poland, and the Citroen car, to be built in conjunction with a Romanian firm, will be sold through these firms' normal distribution channels and, presumably, at prices which do not undercut other models from the same firms.

The question of Soviet and Eastern European home sales becomes less significant after the preceding discussion. For if the Eastern bloc planners are determined to remain net car exporters, there will be no significant Western European exports (of fully assembled models, at least) in the foreseeable future to those countries. The best that Western firms can hope for under these circumstances should be participation in some further expansion plans — albeit at the cost of subsequent greater import threats from the same source. (A minor qualification to this view comes from the 1981 sale of 10,000 Toyota and Mitsubishi cars in East Germany. These cars were imported to offset the effect of the USSR dropping 15,000 Lada exports to East Germany because of widening trade deficit between the COMECON satellite and the USSR. There is precedent for cars being paid for in kind — in 1977 10,000 VW Golf cars were paid for in machinery — but it is unlikely that Japanese firms would wish to pursue this way of doing business[1].)

---

1. "East Germany is planning to buy cars from Japan", *F.T.,* 5:5:81.

TABLE 5.4

DENSITY DEVELOPMENT, SELECTED EASTERN EUROPEAN COUNTRIES
(per 1000)

	USSR	Czechoslovakia	E.Germany	Hungary
1976	19	101	112	55
1980	31	127	149	85

	Poland	Yugoslavia	Bulgaria	Romania
1976	85	72	23	7
1980	60		56	11

1976: MVMA

1980: Fabrimetal

As a matter of interest it is nonetheless interesting to look briefly at the density of car ownership in some Eastern European countries. Table 5.4 reproduces the available evidence for a few years for some countries. Although the data is bound to be unreliable, there is no escaping the general impression that density remains extremely low. Even the most motorized of these countries, East Germany, had by 1980 a density which was surpassed by virtually all Western European countries by the late 1940s. In the USSR density remains at one of the lowest levels in the world. By all accounts the current five-year plan of the USSR (1981-85) has provided for some change in the distribution of resources towards consumer goods (both durables such as cars and non-durables such as foodstuffs). Yet even a sustained shift in the pattern of resource allocation will have barely a perceptible impact upon density of car ownership in this decade. In the USSR, if not most COMECON states, the 1980s will remain a period in which the primacy of public transport is unchallenged.

Chapter Six

The Developing Countries: Reluctant Importers

Given that sales are forecast to grow at only modest rates in the majority of developed country markets for the rest of the decade (and, indeed, beyond) and that, for different reasons, sales in COMECON states are also to remain constrained (see Chapter Five), the developing countries remain the major growth areas to be investigated. To many commentators this sounds unpromising from the start. The well-reported problems of mounting debt, dearth of aid, and urban underemployment suggest a picture of unreliable gloom as far as marketing expensive consumer durables is concerned. In fact nothing could be further from the truth. As has been pointed out[1], many developing countries are already substantial economies, with consumer markets approaching in size those in some of the less affluent mature countries. Moreover, from the point of view of future growth, what should concern car industry planners looking at these countries is that historical precedent suggests that car demand, once initiated, will tend to grow considerably faster than income itself. Thus, for instance, at levels of per capita income of around $1,000 per annum, where Tunisia, Syria, Jordan and Morocco are now placed, car purchasing may grow four times as quickly as GDP per capita. A country experiencing real GDP per capita growth of 7% will see its total income double in ten years, but may see car ownership grow much more strongly, from 15 cars per 1,000 people to say 120 in the same period. The tables in the appendix show the size of the car population in each developing country in 1981, while Table 6.1 shows, in summary form, the relative weights of the car populations by continent. It transpires that the developing countries together (defined to exclude South Africa) account for some 32.84 million cars, or approximately 10.4% of the world total. Of this total, more than half (or 18.15 million) are to be found in Central and South America. Table 6.2 shows the estimated densities of car ownership implied for each continent by these figures, and Table 6.3 lists the developing countries into sub-groups according to their estimated 1980 car ownership densities.

Before proceeding, it is worth noting some of the problems involved with developing country data. First, some of the countries listed here, being in a state of war or other severe disturbances, cannot be relied upon to collect accurate car parc figures. Thus the figures for, say, Lebanon or Uganda must be treated as only broad indicators of magnitudes. Second, some of the very small developing countries, such as Reunion, give misleading density figures suggesting a far greater level of maturity in car consumption than other socio-economic criteria would point to. Again, these cases (most of which have in fact been left out of the tables) must be approached cautiously. Third, there is a universal problem with assessing the rate at which cars are scrapped or abandoned. In countries where formal scrappage requires that a tax

---

1. *The Third World Economic Handbook,* Euromonitor 1982.

TABLE 6.1

CAR POPULATIONS, BY CONTINENT, 1980

Continent	Number of cars	%
N.America	130,785,000	41.5
W.Europe	101,789,981	32.3
E.Europe	18,761,496	6.0
Africa	5,568,060	1.8
(Africa excluding S.Africa)	3,237,152	
Middle East	4,322,009	1.4
Far East	26,942,683	8.6
(Far East excluding Japan)	4,275,386	
Pacific	7,158,275	2.3
(Pacific excluding Australia)	1,445,765	
Caribbean	1,402,692	0.4
Central & South America	18,153,164	5.8
WORLD TOTAL	318,831,620	100.0

TABLE 6.2

DENSITY OF CAR OWNERSHIP BY CONTINENT, 1980
(cars per 1,000 inhabitants)

Asia*	13
Africa	14
Caribbean	14
Latin America	18
Europe	154
(of which EEC**	333)
Oceania	333
(USA	556)
World	**75**

*including Japan
**excluding Greece

TABLE 6.3

DEVELOPING COUNTRIES: DENSITY OF CAR OWNERSHIP BY GROUP, 1980

Density 1-20/1,000

Angola	Malawi	Zambia	Bangladesh
Benin	Mali	Turkey	Burma
Burundi	Mauritania	Bolivia	China
Cameroon	Mozambique	Cuba	India
CA Republic	Niger	Dom.Republic	Indonesia
Chad	Nigeria	Ecuador	Iraq
Congo	Senegal	Haiti	Kampuchea
Egypt	Somalia	Honduras	Rep.Korea
Equat.Guinea	Sudan	Jamaica	Laos
Ethiopia	Swaziland	Nicaragua	Pakistan
Ghana	Tanzania	Paraguay	Philippines
Guinea	Togo	Peru	Sri Lanka
Ivory Coast	Tunisia	Salvador	Syria
Kenya	Uganda	Papua N.Guinea	Taiwan
Liberia	U.Volta	Afghanistan	Thailand
Madagascar	Zaire	UAE	N.Yemen

Density 21-50/1,000

Algeria	Sierra Leone	Costa Rica	Hong Kong
Djibouti	Zimbabwe	Dominica	Iran
Gabon	Belize	Guatemala	Jordan
Mauritius	Chile	Guyana	Malaysia
Morocco	Colombia	Panama	Oman
		Fiji	Sarawak

Density 51-75/1,000

Guinea-Bissau	Brazil	Surinam	Saudi Arabia
Seychelles	Mexico	Uruguay	Singapore

Density 76-100/1,000

Botswana	Gambia	(S.Africa)	Barbados
		Antigua	Venezuela

Density   100/1,000

Argentina	Neths.Antilles	Brunei	Qatar
Bahamas	P.Rico	Israel	Sabah
Bermuda	Tr.& Tobago	Kuwait	Libya
Monserrat	Bahrain	Lebanon	Reunion

or other certification be completed, there is likely to be under-declaring of car obsolescence and consequent over-estimation of the size of the car parc and thus of density. Finally, there are a few particularly anomolous cases where laws or customs seriously affect density. In Libya, for instance, the last economic development plan proposed that every family in the country should be supplied with its own car. Thus the relatively high density shown here (133) reflects government car purchases at least as much as private demand.

As Table 6.4 indicates, sales in certain developing countries were relatively less affected by the 1980-81 recession than were sales in developed countries. The Latin American countries tended to suffer the worst declines in sales, a fact which no doubt reflects the very poor performance of the economies of the continent. Data from ECLA suggest that Latin American GDP grew by only 1.2% in 1981, as compared with 5.8% growth in 1980. The 1981 result was the worst for 35 years, while the region's total current account deficit grew to $34 billion from $28 billion the preceding year. Car sales in Argentina collapsed particularly badly, from 250,200 in 1980 to 176,200 units, with output down 36% to 139,400 units, and vehicle exports (including commercial vehicles) down 93% in volume to a mere 256 units, the entire industry was in severe difficulty. Brazil saw an even larger decline in sales volume, of 40%, following the unprecedented economic difficulties there, after several consequent years of sales in excess of 800,000 units. Elsewhere in the continent, Uruguay saw rapid sales growth, as did Mexico. Other developing countries, notably Libya in Africa and Taiwan in Asia, helped pull up the total for these countries. For the 29 countries listed here, sales only slipped modestly, by approximately 7.7%, between 1980 and 1981.

As far as trade in cars is concerned, the developing countries remain overwhelmingly importers. From a value of $5.8 billion in 1979 imports grew to $28.5 billion in 1980[1], while in 1979 their car exports were only valued at $1.7 billion. This growing deficit with the developed world in car trade is a subject of considerable concern to many governments in developing countries. For, to the extent that fast growth of real disposable income is reflected in sharp rises in consumer durables imports, such as those of cars, balance of trade constraints and even physical congestion at ports, become serious problems. The case of Nigeria was in the 1970s one of the most unfortunate in this respect. Although small assembly plants were established, their late arrival, high unit cost and relatively poor reliability reputations did nothing to stem the flood of imports, particularly of luxury cars. Indeed, in 1980 it was noticeable that Nigeria's car imports were more than four times the volume of any other African state's (excluding South Africa), at 92,600 units, and accounted for 38% of the African total (again, South Africa excluded).

From Table 6.5 it is clear that Japanese manufacturers are the dominant force at present in developing country markets, selling, in 1980, 56% of all cars exported to such markets. The French firms came second in aggregate terms, selling, with a volume of 222,000 units, some 15% of all cars imported. Closer examination of the

---

1. The 1980 figure includes trade in components.

TABLE 6.4

SALES OF CARS IN SELECTED DEVELOPING COUNTRIES, 1978-1981

Country	1978	1979	1980	1981
Egypt	17,200	17,700	21,600	19,000
Libya	55,600	60,300	19,200	75,000
Ivory Coast	17,200	14,800	16,400	12,400
Nigeria	79,000	62,310	108,100	137,000
Kenya	9,400	4,400	6,800	1,600
South Africa	204,700	213,000	277,100	301,000
Zaire	940	1,000	1,250	1,800
Argentina	142,200	195,000	250,200	176,200
Brazil	837,000	864,200	819,200	460,000
Chile	36,200	39,000	63,000	91,470
Colombia	29,000	32,800	43,000	35,500
Uruguay	7,850	13,800	21,000	25,300
Venezuela	107,400	98,000	103,000	99,800
Mexico	231,000	272,000	293,000	351,000
Puerto Rico	63,200	64,000	63,000	70,460
Hong Kong	27,000	31,000	42,000	28,000
India	35,000	29,600	31,000	32,000
Indonesia	19,060	18,000	34,000	37,000
Malaysia	75,400	70,100	97,300	100,000
Philippines	35,250	35,100	30,400	29,600
South Korea	70,400	88,000	44,300	50,590
Taiwan	57,000	75,000	70,300	98,500
Thailand	27,200	25,400	22,600	30,000
Iran	147,000	37,000	72,460	94,700
Iraq	5,100	25,120	45,900	54,900
Kuwait	36,000	33,900	36,200	31,400
Pakistan	13,200	11,710	13,280	7,200
Saudi Arabia	134,000	134,000	171,000	147,000
UA Emirates	23,260	27,030	29,600	29,900

Japanese firms' performance indicates that it is their neighbouring markets of the Far East that their dominance is most complete, with 80% of the import market taken by them in 1980. The developing Pacific area follows close behind, with 78% of all imported cars sold there being sourced in Japan. Between them the six largest country sources (France, Italy, Japan, UK, USA and West Germany) account for 95% of all car exports to developing countries.

TABLE 6.5

DEVELOPING COUNTRIES' CAR IMPORTS, 1980, BY VOLUME AND MAIN SOURCES

	total	% of total
Developing Africa	245,855	16.6
Developing Far East	291,345	19.6
Middle East	463,202	31.2
Developing Pacific	78,964	5.3
Caribbean	121,086	8.2
Central & South America	283,217	19.1
Developing countries' total	1,483,669	100.0

Main Sources

	France	Italy	Japan	UK	USA	West Germany
Developing Africa	109,053	21,365	78,302	19,807	1,090	14,582
Developing Far East	4,394	4,228	233,514	27,337	4,293	13,171
Middle East	22,699	28,092	248,679	78,055	44,623	14,614
Developing Pacific	3,892	480	61,466	11,412	198	1,386
Caribbean	6,666	1,110	103,702	4,438	3,201	1,387
Central & South America	75,187	14,914	108,296	4,654	21,947	18,169
Developing countries' total	221,891	70,189	833,959	145,703	75,352	63,309

The alternative to massive and continued importation of fully assembled cars is, of course, some form of local assembly and/or manufacture. Local output can be substituted for imports as a way of satisfying this nascent demand, while in the process nourishing a wide range of supplier firms. Car exports in turn could thereby be made to yield more than the 3% of LDCs' export earnings which they presently represent, while the 3.6% of total manufacturing output that the car industry currently accounts for in developing countries (less than half the share recorded in the developed countries) could also yield employment rewards. Table 6.6 shows the main production locations at present. The problem of the precise nature and extent of developing country involvement in the car industry naturally arises, of course. Self-sufficiency is one strategy which has had appeal in the past.

TABLE 6.6

MAIN DEVELOPING COUNTRY PASSENGER CAR PRODUCTION LOCATIONS, 1980/1981

	Volume	
	1980	**1981**
Argentina	218,516	139,428
Brazil	983,331	623,900
South Korea	57,225	68,760
India	45,606	42,150
Mexico	303,056	354,900
Colombia	38,274	24,730
Malaysia	81,355	87,800
Peru	10,700	13,100
Philippines	30,186	28,570
Turkey	31,529	25,490
Venezuela	115,965	105,900
Chile	27,530	23,450

Among the earlier experiments in self-sufficiency were the five members of the Andean Pact (Venezuela, Ecuador, Bolivia, Peru and Columbia). Founded in 1969 (when Chile also joined) petrochemicals and car manufacture were identified as two of the spearheads of industrialization which would reap substantial economies of scale from having access to a total market of nearly 60 million inhabitants. Although the value of trade between the members of the group has grown considerably, the car project is not promising. The five members attempted to share out manufacturing tasks among themselves, but renegotiations were soon requested, and bilateral agreements within the membership compromised the principles of the common market. It is clear already that when the members' cars do come onstream, they will be of obsolete design, will be relatively expensive and consequently will require constant protection.

In practice, it appears unlikely that the governments of the Andean Pact members will sacrifice the interests of their own car consumers to such an extent as to forbid competing car imports. The Andean members may very well, instead, engage in joint ventures with other foreign producers, in the hope of at least rescuing something of their automotive plans.

This example is a useful illustration of the pitfalls facing developing country latecomers to the car business. So great is the expertise by now at the disposal of the longer-established firms that not to involve them in any new car project seems to some observers to be akin to suicide.

The Andean Pact case demonstrates some of the problems which arise with autonomous car projects. The difficulties of technology, cost competitiveness and rigorous project scheduling are among those likely to be mitigated by involving a long-established firm. There is, however, a rather different case for involving the established multi-national car producers in a new manufacturing project. It involves not so much what the multinationals know as whom they know: in other words, it is an argument which rests upon these firms' comparatively good access to foreign markets through their marketing and distribution networks. The selection of Suzuki to produce the Maruti, India's third car, was explained partly in terms of the Indian government's desire to see some Indian-assembled cars exported eventually. To obtain access to the joint venture this was one of the undertakings to which Suzuki had to agree. But elsewhere among the developing countries there are far more significant instances of multinationals' marketing apparatus being called upon to aid the entry of a new supplier into the world car market. Probably the most significant of all is the entry of Taiwan's nascent car industry, and the manner in which the multinational chosen to foster the project will be used.

Competitive bidding between Toyota, Nissan, and Ford's Japanese affiliate, Toyo Kogyo, lasted for some time before the Taiwanese government agency, the Council for Economic Planning and Development, selected Toyota to enter a joint venture worth $500 million with Taiwanese interests. The major Taiwanese stakeholder will be China Steel. The project is the biggest single industrial undertaking in Taiwan in recent years, and follows the government's decision that cars are to be seen as a "strategic industry"[1]. For the first five years the plant will largely sell to the home market, where there are already a number of firms supplying the 80,000/year car market. The mechanics of the joint venture, however, are the important points.

---

1. "Taiwan's car industry: Auto-locomotive", *The Economist,* 6:3:82.

First, the government judged that 200,000 annual unit capacity was needed to reach competitive cost levels. This at once dictated foreign involvement. Given the need to import certain parts, the foreign exchange constraint required that 50% of output be exported. This too pointed to foreign involvement[1]. Balancing the clear need for the Taiwanese to obtain a foreign firm's expertise in these areas, the Taiwanese in return could offer good domestic market growth (from 55,000 cars sold in 1978 to 77,000 in 1979 to 80,000 in 1981) forecast by Ford to reach 130,000 sales by 1984. In addition another point in the Asian matrix of assembly for re-export could be offered to a prospective Japanese partner. The degree of local content was then subject to the usual negotiation, with 70% being the Taiwanese request, with 90% to be aimed at ultimately. This level of local content is likely only to be achievable if Japanese supplier firms set up their own subsidiaries in Taiwan itself.

As for marketing the export surplus, what was paramount for the Taiwanese was securing access to a sophisticated marketing network overseas. As a spokesman of the Council for Economic Planning and Development put it, "we don't want to be confined to Africa and South America ... we want to be able to export worldwide and we want to make sure that the quality is good enough. We don't want to make the same mistakes that Hyundai of Korea made"[2]. The prospective problem of excess capacity worldwide appears not to have deterred the Taiwanese car capacity to 450,000 units.

The evidence to hand at present strongly suggests that joint ventures will be the path chosen by the majority of developing country car industry strategists. But since this choice will itself be conditioned by the developed country-based firms in their pursuit of some form of world car strategy, the eventual outcomes may not be easily predictable. Chapter 7 now goes on to look at the extent to which world car systems might pull the developing countries in closer to the industry.

---

1. "Taiwan seeks role in world auto industry", *Automotive News,* 15:2:82
2. *Automotive News,* ibid.

Chapter Seven

The Developed Countries: Approaching Maturity

The development of car sales in the main markets of Europe since 1945 has exhibited remarkable similarities across countries. This has occurred despite the countries' substantial disparities of physical characteristics, such as dispersion of economic activity, population density per acre, extent of urbanization, and disparities in economic conditions such as tax rates and, above all, growth of real income per head. Looking at the eleven major markets in Europe, it transpires that inside a range of five years, from 1968 to 1973, all had achieved densities (i.e. car ownership expressed relative to 1,000 population) of 200. (Sweden is an exception to this, having attained the 250 level.) Although the gap in attaining the 250 density level was rather greater, with Sweden attaining it by 1968 and Finland not until 1981, there was still sufficient homogeneity of experience to suggest that car ownership as a phenomenon must conform to certain basic principles.

The search for principles of this sort has gone on for some time. Before the last war statisticians took considerable interest in identifying the underlying factors driving the car ownership trend. In an article written in 1939, C.F. Roos and V. von Szeliski examined the determinants of car demand[1], and ever since a number of mathematicians and economists, some of them very eminent, have turned their attention to the subject.

For the 1980s, the main question which the car industry faces in this area is to what extent can similar patterns be assumed to persist as densities of car ownership grow ever higher.

At the risk of oversimplifying slightly, all car (and more generally, consumer durable) forecasts can be divided into two categories. The first type is called the trend or logistic function type. In these, it is assumed that the absolute level of car ownership rises gradually from a base at or close to zero. As ownership picks up it enters a period of rapid and then accelerating expansion before slowing and eventually reaching saturation, from which no further growth takes place. Graphically, these models form the familiar flattened S-shaped curve. The important point about these models is that they make no allowance for deviations in such economic variables as income per capita, income distribution, or the price of cars relative to other goods. They are essentially mathematical models.

Such models have been used to predict UK car sales since 1962 by the Transport

---

1. "Factors governing changes in domestic automobile demand", in *The Dynamics of Automobile Demand*, G.M. Corporation, 1939.

and Road Reseach Laboratory (TRRL), and are shown in Chart 4. But such models were found early on to over-predict consistently the rate at which car sales grew. The search for variants then began, and two were established. The simpler change was to allow the curve a degree of non-linearity in its connection between the absolute level of car ownership and the growth rate of ownership. This meant that growth from zero to half the saturation level could be arrived at faster than the second half was achieved. This was found to improve, but still not perfect, the model's fit with the actual results. The second variant led to trend models becoming akin to the second major family of forecasting models — the causal models.

Causal models are conceptually rather different from trend models. Instead of merely extrapolating figures from historical trends, the former look to the factors which might in reality affect households' buying decisions. Real income changes, before and after tax, along with real car prices, relative to other goods' prices, and the cost of running cars are the main factors used in such work. The difference in design between these models is thus that while trend models seek to answer the question "what will happen?" directly, causal models answer it indirectly by first asking "how will it happen?".

Advocates of causal models tend to point to three arguments for their supremacy. First, experience with British data suggests that while persistent over-prediction in car sales using trend models can be reduced by adding income and price factors, causal models have in some cases been more accurate. Second, trend models need a saturation level to be fixed a priori before they can work. Yet controversy rages over the appropriate level for this parameter. Some British sources believe 600 is attainable[1]. While the exact figure chosen for saturation need not critically affect the model's accuracy, such a wide divergence of views on the "correct" saturation level suggests that interpreting movements away from trend is difficult. Finally, it has been argued that causal models are by their nature better suited to giving explicit recognition to such factors as company car sales, household composition, the impact of public transport, and changing fuel costs. Given the growing weight of opinion that such factors do affect density developments (e.g. "good public transport helps curb the increase in car ownership"[2]) there may be a case for being able to introduce such factors formally into the forecasting process.

The obvious elements of such a model are income, expressed in various ways, and car prices. A number of income variables such as pre-tax, real and nominal, and household and individual, have been tested in some studies. Real personal disposable income was found to be the most significant variable in one study[3]; while later tests

1. See P.Mullen and M.White, "Forecasting Car Ownership — a New Approach" in *Traffic Engineering and Control,* Vol.18, no.9, September 1977.
2. TRRL Report no.541, "Subsidization of Public Transport", 1980.
3. *The Demand for New Cars: An Econometric Model for Short-term Forecasting,* National Economic Development Office (NEDO), London, 1974.

CHART 4

FORECASTS OF CAR OWNERSHIP MADE BETWEEN 1962 AND 1978
Cars per person: Great Britain

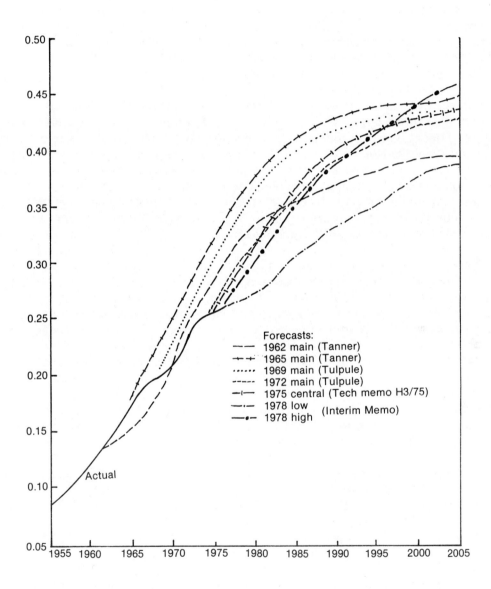

Forecasts:
- —— 1962 main (Tanner)
- —+—+ 1965 main (Tanner)
- ·········· 1969 main (Tulpule)
- ------ 1972 main (Tulpule)
- —⊢— 1975 central (Tech memo H3/75)
- —·—· 1978 low   (Interim Memo)
- —•— 1978 high

Actual

found that "car purchasing income" was the strongest explanation of car purchase[1]. (In this variant, defined as income relative to average car prices, a 1% fall in car prices relative to all other goods is equivalent to a 1% rise in income, relative to the general price level.) Further work has shown that the minimum hire purchase deposit reached for a car purchase is also significant[2].

No systematic work has been carried out on company car purchases. Although it has been recognised that this factor must have a major effect on British sales[3] and fleet sales do dominate the total — some 60%-65% — it is not clear how this factor might affect density development in the future. One stockbroker's analyst has estimated, however, that the adoption of realistic taxation of all company car benefits to drivers would cut new registrations by 10% and cut ownership per 1,000 people by 5.5% by 1985[4]. Certainly to the extent that fleet sales reflect, in part, the higher real cost of cars in Britain than elsewhere in developed countries[5], and also the tax system, changes in the latter might cut the appeal of company cars. This would have a complex effect upon the number of new private sales as some of the erstwhile company cars would presumably be sold to their users. There would probably also be an impact on the mix of demand. Finally, the marked tendency for fleet purchasers to be of UK-sourced cars (including own-brand imports such as some Vauxhalls and Fords) suggest that car import patterns would be altered too, at least in the short-run[6]. This fact is, indeed, thought to have figured in BL and other British firms' submissions to the Treasury on company car taxation reform.

Obviously, all developed countries have public transport provisions. So what is relevant for car sales forecasting is whether the nature and/or cost of such provision has a significant effect upon sales. Once again, little work has been done on the topic, other than to note the omission. Thus, "our present lack of evidence concerning the magnitude of the effect of public transport on car ownership is no justification for assuming it has no effect as present forecasts do"[7]. The same authors have also asked whether including public transport provisions in a sales forecast will merely slow the rate of car ownership growth, or also influence the ultimate saturation level itself. Two issues which have, however, received some attention are the effect of car ownership on bus patronage in the UK, and the effect of transport subsidy on public transport usage. On the first point, samples appear to point to a clear inverse relationship: in 1976, roughly speaking, each new car on the road cut 300

---

1. "A Disaggregate model of Household Car Ownership", Departments of Transport, Environment and Transport, Research Report no.20, 1978.

2. NEDO, op.cit.

3. e.g. G.E.Giles and T.E.Worsley.

4. Simon and Coates report, cited in *Financial Times* Survey of Company Cars, Jan.5, 1981.

5. For evidence see "Big Variations Between European Car Prices". *Financial Times* Survey, May 19, 1981.

6. But recent work shows that more than half the fleet-owning companies surveyed in 1981 had one or more foreign cars in their fleet. See "Companies Turn to Foreign Makers", *The Times* 24:7:81.

7. Mullen & White, op.cit.

bus trips per year of UK bus demand. The growth of car ownership over 1964-76 is estimated to have been associated with about 45% of the drop in bus patronage over the same period[1]. Of course, it is the reverse causation which is of more interest here. On that issue, the only evidence is hazy, but suggests that even extremely cheap and frequent bus services cannot easily entice urban car-drivers to leave their cars, let alone not buy a car in the first place[2]. On the question of subsidy, cross-country data is available, and shows that the UK has not experienced a greater than average rise in public transport subsidies as a percent of operating costs. By 1975 the UK appeared to be a fairly low-subsidy country in this respect[3]. Moreover, even if subsidies were larger, an OECD study suggests that a given rise in subsidy would result in a response in public transport usage only one-third as large[4]. Thus, what evidence exists seems to suggest firstly that UK public transport does not enjoy a greater than average degree of subsidy, and secondly that even if it did, this would probably have a small effect on car usage. Given, furthermore, the weak link between car ownership and the portion of usage which is susceptible to transport policy, it seems unlikely that transport policy will significantly affect UK car sales patterns.

If car running costs were found in many studies to be significant in affecting car purchase (either its volume or mix) and the UK were likely to witness a different evolution of running costs to other countries, this item would be an important component of a causal model of sales forecasting. On neither point, however, is the evidence strong. First, four different studies, carried out between 1974 and 1980, have each failed to find running costs important, either as a determinant of purchases or usage. A revision of the TRRL long-term forecasts, made in the light of the fuels uncertainty in 1974, failed to find any significant link between purchase and running costs[5]. Two further studies, in 1974 and 1978, also found virtually no connection[6,7], with one report commenting, "the variable for running costs proved insignificant, and it was decided to omit any version of the variables relating to running costs." And a more detailed appraisal in 1980 confirmed that a 1% rise in real fuel prices yielded only a 0.10 to 0.17% fall in kilometers travelled per car during the 1972-78 sample period[8]. Moreover, studies of car mileage by year (reproduced in Chart 5) show very little response through time to fuel cost changes. Looking at the volume of passenger car traffic over a longer period to find evidence of a clear impact from higher petrol prices gives equally clear results. Chart 6 shows car and taxi travel, expressed as thousands of million kilometers, over the period 1969-79, ranged against two cost indices: The

---

1. TRRL Report No.872, "Effect of Car Ownership on Bus Patronage", 1979.

2. K.Bhatt, "The Influence of Pricing on Travel Behaviour and Model Choice", Background Paper no.4(b), *Urban Transport and the Environment*, OECD, Paris, 1979.

3. TRRL Report No.541, op.cit.

4. TRRL Report No.541, op.cit.

5. See, e.g., "Hard Times Ahead in Train and Bus Travel", *Financial Times,* 4 Sept.1980; "Councils Told to Control Costs of Local Transport", *The Times,* 25 Sept.1980.

6. NEDO, op.cit.

7. Dept. of Transport, op.cit.

8. TRRL Report no.593, "Effect of Fuel Prices on Traffic", 1980.

CHART 5

INDEX OF VEHICLE KM PER CAR, 1972-1978 (Oct. 1972 = 100), Great Britain

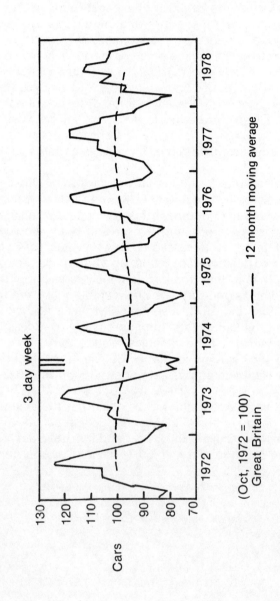

Automobile Association's car usage costs series (expressed as pence per mile) and the retail price of petrol (expressed as pence per gallon). Simply by inspection, one can see that the effect of the rise in retail petrol prices late in 1973 had a modest and short-lived effect upon distances driven. Between calendar 1973 and 1974 the fall in the total distance driven by private car (and taxi) was only 2.9%. Thereafter, the expansion of traffic growth has been slightly less rapid than before 1973, but a portion of this can almost certainly be explained by the lower growth rate of GNP in the subsequent years.

Comparison of countries' retail price index weightings would reveal whether car running costs had moved sufficiently differently between countries to justify further attention. But, in any case, no UK study has found a sufficiently close relationship between such costs and either intensity of car use or car purchase to make the effort worthwhile. This is not, however, necessarily to deny that the changing level and composition of running costs has a negligible effect upon the car industry as far as manufacturers are concerned. For the finding that travelling in the UK is relatively inelastic with respect to petrol price rises does not preclude the possibility that changing running costs may be associated with significant shifts in demand between car segments, and with changes in the pattern of new car buying and/or scrappage. Only a little evidence throws light directly on this issue. One study of import penetration in British car sales found in 1976 that fuel economy was not an important factor in raising a model's market share, given other model characteristics[1].

The foregoing discussion suggests that the case for believing that influences on car ownership and new car purchasing, other than straightforward income factors, is by no means proven. Obviously there will be periods when extraneous factors, such as new taxes, physical petrol shortages, etc., will critically affect the market. But the overwhelming body of evidence linking income per head to car ownership is likely to continue to hold for the future. What is equally likely, however, is that the link will diminish in intensity. Experience with countries as they develop and generate progressively higher levels of real per capita living standards shows that the tendency to spend more money on cars decreases. Expressed as the ratio between extra income and extra car purchasing, the income elasticity of demand falls. It can fall below unity, indeed, so that a 3% rise in real household disposable income in a mature economy may be associated with only a 1.5% rise in spending, in real terms, on cars.

This is by and large common ground between car firms and outside analysts. Typical of the more recent forecasts offered is that of Toyota, who posit 2.1% growth in car demand annually between 1985 and 1990, after 4.2% growth in the 1970s. In Europe and the US they foresee 1-2% annual average growth; for Africa 5-7% and for the Middle East growth in excess of 10%.

Is this sufficient of a drop to cause consternation to the world's car producers?

---

1. J.Cubbin and D.Leech, "Import Penetration in the UK Passenger Car Market: A Cross Section Study for 1975, Warwick University Economic Research Papers, No.88, June 1976.

CHART 6

TRAVEL BY CAR AND TAXI, UK, 1969-1979
(thousand million km), with AA cost of car usage and petrol price series.

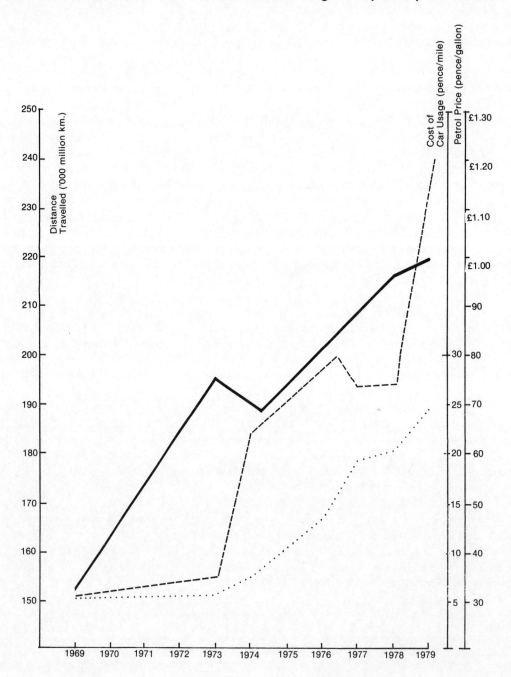

No. First, it has long been anticipated that a deceleration in growth would come about — indeed, for most people in the industry, the surprise is not that it is likely to come about but that it is coming about so late. In the 1930s forecasters were talking of saturation in the US car market setting in at a level of density of 200 per 1,000 people. It is now on course for three times that level. Second, it must be borne in mind that 2% annual growth on top of a mature market, such as the US million unit market, represents, in absolute terms, a substantial extra volume of output. In the US, for instance, this implies 180,000 extra sales per year, compound. Finally, the scope may exist within the volume sales growth just outlined to increase the value of each unit. The "more car per car" strategy aims at pushing up further the level of equipment sold in each unit, not only to enhance the wholesale and retail price but also to entice buying of the parts of the car — the options — on which the profit has, by tradition, always been disproportionately high.

If this is the type of future the industry faces, where do "world car" strategies fit in? Can they help in the move toward the "more car per car" path, for instance, or is their rationale at root much simpler — to help erode the firm's cost base while fighting a tougher battle internationally with foreign firms at the retail level?

Chapter Eight

The World Car in the 1980s

I An overview of the world car concept

The world car concept has, at least implicitly, been in existence for several years now. Writing of the rapid integration of the European manufacturers' operations and the substantial growth of intra EEC trade in cars after the Treaty of Rome was signed in 1958, Mira Wilkins, a noted historian of the industry, observed that, "the economic integration of the world automobile industry has been encouraged by the product offerings of multinational corporations that have moved away from cars, and more particularly from parts, designed for narrowly circumscribed home markets ... The potential for transnational sources of supplies and markets has grown. Even countries in Europe outside the Common Market, Spain for example, can be involved in an integrated market. Ford's Fiesta, introduced in September 1976, is properly called a European car; it is a product of no single country"[1]. A few years later, Lee Iococca, then chairman of Chrysler, predicted how, after a shaking-out period in which many well-known car firms would cease production, "the goal of all auto companies will be the same ... to find the right combination of manufacturing plants, markets and dealer-distribution networks worldwide that will produce the lowest costs and highest profits ... it will be a global shakeout equal in scope to the consolidation of the US auto industry after world war one"[2].

Other commentators have agreed along broadly similar lines. A special issue of "Ward's Auto World" published in May 1981 took the view that world cars would become the norm, produced at rates of at least 2 million units annually. To achieve this, "partnerships are becoming a must for survival. The alternative is slow death for those who fail to enter the partner hunt." Concluding that, "like the earth itself, the auto world keeps shrinking," the review saw the pooling of resources between car firms seen so far as but "the tip of an iceberg that must grow". Yet other commentators dismiss the connection between world cars as a way of keeping competitive and a wave of inter-firm mergers. No less an authority than the managing director of Toyota Motor Sales argued early in 1982 that mergers were neither a necessary consequence of, nor precondition for, world car production. There was, nonetheless, no doubt that there would be "an unprecedented push to use new technologies and new materials ... and the introduction of so-called world cars made from components produced on a vast scale"[3].

---

1. M.Wilkins, "Multinational Automobile Enterprises and Regulation: An Historical Overview", in D.H.Ginsberg & W.J.Abernathy (eds.) *Government, Technology and the Future of the Automobile*, (McGraw-Hill, New York, 1980).
2. "Carmakers see "World Motors" in their future", *Washington Post,* 5:4:81.
3. "Car industry in second industrial revolution", *Financial Times,* 3:3:82.

To understand the basis of the world car concept, and to be able to criticise it and identify properly its shortcomings (and, of course its strengths) it is useful to place it in some sort of context. For the idea of assembling cars in several locations does not exist in a vacuum: it is simply a reflection of experiences in other parts of manufacturing industry and from earlier decades. What very few commentators on their car industry's prospects tend to realise is that there is already plenty of analogous experience and evidence to which one may refer. The best-known example of an industry in which production for home consumption tended to be replaced by imports of components for home assembly and ultimately by full foreign assembly is consumer electronics. Radios, televisions and other items are to a large extent imports for most mature economies nowadays. What drove long-established firms to shut down completely or to supplement their home operations with overseas assembly work was cost: the fact that labour costs per unit of output were significantly lower in other locations, such as Mexico or South East Asia. Once quality control had been properly established, it was well within the grasp of a company to transfer parts of its operation overseas, reimporting the final result or at least most of its components.

Attempts to identify patterns in this process and predict which industries may exhibit it next have given rise to a large number of economic studies on what has come to be known as the product-life cycle hypothesis. Extending the hypothesis to the car industry, Professor Wells of Harvard Business School has, over a number of years, come to the view that "the automobile has behaved in the way that the model would forecast (and) the pattern of automotive trade has fit well the forecasts of the product life cycle model." Although, he argues, "the result of the product life cycle is not an inevitable disappearance of the US industry", he does believe that following the evident success of the Japanese export boom, developing country sources will be next in line as suppliers to the American and European markets[1].

Obviously, the implications of this are of the utmost importance for the industry. Will in fact GM, Ford, BL and others go the way of countless firms in the textiles, clothing or radio industries? And so quickly? The next sections of this chapter attempt to answer these questions.

The best way to begin answering the questions about the future of the world car concept that were raised at the end of the last section is to enumerate first the forces which will be pressing towards the development of world cars, and then the constraints which those forces will meet. In the light of this discussion the type of world cars that may be expected to typify manufacturers' plans later in the decade may then be defined more closely.

The first impulse behind the adoption of world cars to a greater extent by western car firms must be the more intense degree of price and non-price competition felt from the Japanese. Initially, as Chapter 2 indicated, Japanese cars were sold on price

---

1. L.T.Wells, "The International Product Life Cycle and US Regulation of the Automobile Industry", in Ginsburg & Abernathy, op.cit.

alone; now many of their other characteristics are also preferred. Studies have demonstrated the extent of the Japanese firms' cost differential, and this is examined later in this chapter. The importance of enhanced competition lies in its implications that more use of low-cost locations for components and assembly should be used, and on the face of it this should lead directly to a world car orientation.

Second, the extent of government involvement in the industry is very likely to grow, as suggested in Chapter 1. It is simply too important a sector for governments, increasingly jealous of their economies' jobs, to leave alone. This regulatory mood has implications for local content rules and for the patterns of imports and exports, both of finished cars and of parts, which can be allowed. For the sake of maintaining a sales presence in a market, then, greater resort to a matrix of trade flows may henceforth be necessary.

The constraints on this push towards a more widespread use of the world car concept can in turn be listed under three headings. First, it is crucial for the plan that there should be relatively free international movement of both parts and fully assembled cars. If quotas and other quantitative trade restrictions apply to cars and components, there will be supply and flexibility constraints built into the plan. In addition, as tariff and non-tariff barriers mount, the scope for capricious and changing interpretation becomes greater, so that plans evolved over years may suddenly be jeopardised by administrative decisions. At present the most awkward threat posed to imports of manufactured items arises through the relatively undisciplined resort to Article XIX of the GATT, which allows import barriers to be raised on an offending item or items, but provides no mechanism for the barriers' subsequent removal. Clearly, then, trade policy is an important prerequisite for the successful operation of the world car, and deserves attention accordingly. The second constraint which can face world car planning follows from the first — it is the possibility of governments' industrial policy priorities and decisions — in both developed and developing locations — impeding firms' decisions. The type of industrial policy decisions which could intrude on world car planning would be export floor rules, requiring that a given share of a plant operating in a given country should be exported. Another example would be a requirement that local content (i.e. the proportion of domestically-produced components) should exceed a certain level and be changed through time. Issues of this sort, which already are a characteristic of foreign investment agreements in most developing countries, look as if they may be increasingly common in the west from now on too. They must therefore be examined as a possible barrier to the full realization of world car plans.

A third constraint which may impede progress towards world cars is the heterogeneity of tastes. Evidence has already been presented to show that car firms' product planners must face substantial differences in taste patterns even between neighbouring countries such as France and Germany. But as more countries are involved in the marketing of world cars, a still greater degree of convergence of tastes would be desirable from the producers' point of view. But is this in evidence? Again, this cannot be taken on trust.

II The threats to international trade in cars

As was noted in the introduction, international trade in motor vehicle products has grown very rapidly in the last decade. From totalling $41 billion in 1973 it grew to $98.98 billion in 1978 and $115.36 billion in 1979. Including parts, world automotive trade grew to $127 billion in 1980, after $117 billion in 1979. As table 8.1 indicates, this represents nearly threefold growth over the period. Table 8.2, which is based upon trade figures covering not only full assembled motor vehicles but also parts, shows magnitudes of even greater importance, and highlights further the expansion of Japanese exports.

For the early part of the 1970s, this trade was relatively unconstrained by barriers. Indeed, generally speaking, it was precisely in manufactured goods such as cars that the liberalization impact of the successive post-war GATT conferences had had the greatest impact. Trade for most of the 1960s and 1970s was growing considerably more quickly than output. Over the 1963-73 period, world exports of manufactures grew at an annual average rate of 11%; world output of manufactures grew by 7% per year. In the 1973-80 period, both rates were lower, but trade still outpaced output, with annual average rates of 5% and 3.5% respectively.

As car sales fell, after 1979, however, and, more particularly, as Japanese import penetration rates began to increase, there was more and more resort to quotas and other forms of non-tariff barrier to restrict the growth of imports. Table 8.3 summarizes, as at mid-1982, the import restrictions applied by the main car importing countries. Sometimes, cars were simply kept standing on docksides while elaborate administrative procedures were carried out; France is known to do this for certain categories of goods, including, in 1981, Japanese cars[1].

Even developing countries with a vested interest in liberalized trade — such as the newly-industrializing states like South Korea and Taiwan — have lately been raising barriers on certain motor vehicle products. In April, the Taiwanese government banned certain heavy-duty tractor imports from Japan, having already banned their heavy-duty trucks. Apart from anger over the large ($3.5 billion in 1981) trade deficit with Japan, the Taiwanese were keen to lend "infant industry" protection to the Hua Tung Automotive Corporation, a joint venture with GM[2]. (Later in 1982, GM pulled out of the project).

This phenomenon was, of course, by no means confined to international trade in cars. Writing of the worldwide drift towards more protectionist policies, the World Bank noted in mid-1981 how:-

the 1970s did see one new and disturbing development in trade relations —
a plethora of specific restrictions, introduced in numerous ways. There

---

1. "Paris delays Japan car shipments", *F.T.*, 6:2:81.
2. "Taiwan: An angry neighbor slams a door on Japan", *Business Week,* 19:4:82.

TABLE 8.1

MOTOR VEHICLES: WORLD TRADE BY MAJOR TRADING REGIONS, 1973-1979
(in billions of US dollars)

Origin	Year	Destination					% of total	World	% growth
		North America	Western Europe	Japan	Oil exporting developing countries	Non-oil exporting developing countries			
N.America	1973	8.77	0.52	0.09	0.37	0.85		10.84	
	1978	16.58	1.11	0.18	2.25	1.99		22.66	
	1979	17.37	1.46	0.23	2.09	5.53	21.2	24.41	2.25
W.Europe	1973	3.68	14.25	0.09	0.99	1.91		22.03	
	1978	5.89	34.38	0.34	4.01	4.31		50.86	
	1979	6.70	44.08	0.44	4.02	5.25	54.4	62.76	2.85
Japan	1973	2.53	0.76	—	0.34	0.78		4.90	
	1978	8.94	2.92	—	2.67	3.00		19.03	
	1979	10.11	3.56	—	2.34	3.16	17.9	20.69	4.22
Non-oil exporting countries	1973	0.10	0.02	—	0.02	0.24		0.38	
	1978	0.28	0.17	0.01	0.30	0.50		1.37	
	1979	0.33	0.23	0.01	0.35	0.60	1.4	1.65	4.34
Other[1]	1973	0.01		0.18	1.72			2.85	
	1978	0.06		0.52	9.23			5.06	
	1979	0.65		0.67	8.81		5.1	5.85	
World	1973	15.09	15.55	0.18	1.72	3.78		41.00	
	1978	31.75	38.58	0.52	9.23	9.80		98.98	
	1979	35.16	49.33	0.67	8.81	14.54	100.0	115.36	2.81

Sources: GATT, *International Trade 1978/79*, *International Trade 1979/80*, *International Trade 1980/81*.

1. includes light commercial vehicles as well as passenger cars.

TABLE 8.2

INDUSTRIAL COUNTRIES' EXPORTS OF MOTOR VEHICLES AND PARTS, 1979-1980
(billion dollars)

Origin	Year	North America	Japan	Western Europe	EC(9)	Industrial countries	Developing countries	World
N.America	1979	19.5	0.2	1.8	1.5	21.4	5.6	27.8
	1980	17.4	0.2	1.8	1.4	19.4	6.4	26.6
U.S.	1979	10.0	0.2	1.7	1.4	12.0	5.0	16.9
	1980	8.8	0.2	1.7	1.4	10.8	5.6	17.0
Japan	1979	9.6	—	3.2	2.4	12.8	5.8	20.1
	1980	12.1	—	4.2	3.0	16.3	8.7	27.0
W.Europe	1979	7.4	0.5	48.0	37.6	55.8	10.5	68.7
	1980	7.6	0.4	49.4	38.5	57.4	13.4	73.4
EEC(9)	1979	6.8	0.5	43.3	34.1	50.5	9.5	62.1
	1980	6.9	0.4	44.1	34.5	51.4	12.2	65.9
Industrial countries	1979	36.4	0.7	53.0	41.5	90.1	21.8	116.6
	1980	37.0	0.6	55.4	42.9	93.1	28.5	126.9

Source: UN, trade data tapes.

TABLE 8.3

RESTRICTIONS ON JAPANESE CAR SALES IN DEVELOPED COUNTRIES, 1981/2

United Kingdom	10-11% market share ceiling, dating from 1975 package to nationalize BL
Federal Republic of Germany	Growth limit of 10% pa on 1980 sales (252,000 units)
Netherlands	No increase on 1980 level
Luxembourg	No increase on 1980 level
Italy	Quota of 2,400 units
France	3% market share ceiling
Belgium	Reduction of 7% on 1980 sales
EEC as a whole	Common External Tariff is 10.9%
Canada	Shipments of "around 174,000" units as against 158,000 in 1980
Australia	All imports restricted to 20% of market. Tariff of 57%. Local content must be 85% to count as home-produced
USA	Shipments of 1.68mn for 1981 (Japanese fiscal year). Subsequent shipment limits to be calculated taking account of US market conditions. Tariff is 2.9%
Denmark Greece Ireland	No restrictions
Japan	No quotas or tariffs on assembled cars, but internal taxes, depending on engine size. Distribution and administrative checking systems alleged to operate as non-tariff barriers.

NOTE: The Benelux and Canadian restrictions are supposed to last only for 1981. The others appear to be more permanent.

were serious trade disputes between the USA, the EEC and Japan over steel and automobile trade . . . The key to maintaining an open trading system is for each industrial country to come to grips with the opportunity and the challenge which adjusting to a changing international environment involves.

Similar points, made in connection with the car industry itself, arose in the latest report from GATT:-

"In explaining the nature of this we may begin by noting the tendency for protectionism to spread by sectoral arrangements. This tendency is most difficult to arrest for economic as well as political reasons. It is well known, not least to industrialists themselves, that the grant of protection to an industry necessarily reduces the competitiveness of some other industry or industries, making them demand protection in turn . . .

This causal relationship can best be illustrated by the effect of protection enjoyed by some basic semi-manufacturing industry on all the downstream industries. Given that steel represents some 18% of the value of a finished automobile, it is clear that the steel price increased in the United States and the EC, consequent on the arrangements adopted in 1978 with respect to imports of steel, compounded the difficulty experienced by the automobile industries of these two markets in their competition with Japanese producers."[1]

There is, moreover, little likelihood of these forces against freer trade diminishing until unemployment in western countries at least begins to level off. With OECD countries' joblessness equivalent in 1981 to 6.8% of their total labour force, as against 5.8% in 1980 and 5.1% in 1979, and demographic factors due to push up the labour force very quickly for the next four years or more, labour market slack will not abate rapidly, whatever happens to the pace of the economic recovery expected to gain momentum from 1982.

There are two relevant points about this hesitancy in developed countries' commitment to relatively free trade in manufactured goods, as far as the car industry's plans for the 1980s are concerned. The first concerns the ambitions of certain developing country producers, notably those in Taiwan, to become significant exporters to the west during this decade. Will these plans now be seriously compromised? The same point might be raised in connection with the Eastern European producers, whose exports are discussed in Chapter 5. But the second point is potentially of far greater importance for the established western car producers, and in particular for their evolving "world car" plans. This is the question: how far can a threat to the untrammelled movement of components and fully assembled cars, upon which the strategies of the world car are to a large extent based, undermine the economics of this

---

1. GATT, *International Trade 1980/81.*

strategy?

So far the EEC countries have been unable to agree on a sufficiently united front to apply any community-wide barriers to Japanese car imports. Since three current members — Greece, Ireland and Denmark — have no car capacity of their own, they have no desire to see their citizens' choice of cars constrained. The Dutch position is ambivalent too[1]. Moreover, the commitment of the German authorities to any rigorous protectionism is never whole-hearted[2]. Few observers believe that a concerted EEC front against Japanese cars will ever be mounted.

In a late turn in the debate over the appropriate level of protection which their car firms need, European governments and industry spokesmen have come to stress local content rules. A recent example involves the Japanese involvement in assembly and component exchanges in the UK and Australia. In the first case, the BL Triumph Acclaim, which possesses about 30% Japanese parts, according to BL, is threatened by the Italian motor industry with being considered a Japanese car[3]. Claiming that the British content is only 60%, the Italians are anxious not to see their 2,400 cars per year import quota against the Japanese retained. Anticipating similar cases to arise in future (notably if Nissan does eventually establish a plant in the UK) the Italian car firms are keen to set a discouraging precedent for Japanese producers. Acting together through their trade association ANFIA, the Italian producers also want the EC Commission in Brussels to lay down criteria for establishing local content rules. The case is of particular interest to FIAT, since it already feels threatened by the joint venture already announced between fellow Italian producer Alfa Romeo and Nissan, which would also tend to undermine the cost-competitiveness of all-Italian cars.

Given that, within Europe, it is BL which is furthest advanced with cooperation with Japanese firms, it is likely that further BL-Honda ties and the prospective, although now delayed, Nissan plant within Britain will generate a great deal more controversy. At present any car assembled within an EEC member state is counted as being domestically-made, and no formal local content rules exist. As far as EFTA member states are concerned, they can be sold freely within the EEC if they possess at least 60% EEC-sourced content by ex-works value.

A similar case has aroused the interest of the British car industry. In April 1982 it became known that cars assembled in Australia, partly with Japanese components, would be shipped to the UK and would not be counted as part of the UK's informal 11% of the market ceiling on Japanese car imports[4]. As part of their agreement with Japanese producer Mitsubishi, the Australian government encourages exports of just such fully-assembled cars, so as to offset the foreign exchange cost to Australia of importing Japanese components. But in attempting to circumscribe this new source

---

1. ''Dutch opposed to Benelux curb on Japanese cars''. *F.T.,* 16:2:81.
2. ''Europe gives up hope of cut in car imports from Japan'', *F.T.,* 15:5:81.
3. ''Italy questions Acclaim's parentage'', *F.T.,* 26:4:82.
4. ''Japan finds backdoor into Britain'', *Sunday Times,* 25:4:82.

of part-Japanese cars, the British motor industry and the government realise that they might undermine the case they are simultaneously preparing, to have BL cars with a substantial Japanese content admitted freely to other EC markets. Expressing the issue forcefully, one British industry spokesman argued that, "it does not matter whether the cars come from Australia or Timbuktu, the cars are still Japanese." Trade union organizations among the European car-producing countries have taken a similar view, for example, at a conference held in April 1982, at which representatives of 3.9 million car workers all over the world were present[1]. The British union position predates this considerably; in April 1980 the National Executive of the Labour Party voted to impose a 40% local content floor on car importers as a priority measure[2].

Partly reflecting pressure from Ford UK, BL, the trade unions involved and the other European car manufacturers, the British government have been particularly keen to see a high level of local content applying to the cars produced at any new Nissan plant in Britain. But the 80% share of local content initially agreed on (building up from an initial 60%) is apparently felt to be low enough to allow Nissan to import all the high technology elements, leaving the more mundane parts such as castings to be built locally[3]. At that level, as the Japanese have pointed out, their cars would still generate more local value added than do many Vauxhall or Ford models which are imported virtually complete[4]. The higher the local content, quite apart from the greater employment spin-offs, the more the overall Japanese cost advantage is whittled away — and the less the scope for predatory price-setting by Nissan in Europe.

A particularly important development over the possible tightening of local content regulations involves the USA. In mid-1982, no fewer than 191 congressmen and 10 senators, strongly backed by the United Auto Workers, introduced a bill to set minimum local content levels for cars sold in the USA. By 1985 they propose that 75% North American (i.e. US and Canadian) content would be demanded from any firm selling over 200,000 cars per year in the USA. Those selling over 500,000 cars per year would face a 90% local content floor[5].

An obvious implication of such local content regulations will be to guarantee a certain floor of production in a low-productivity high-cost country. In the case of the UK, there is little doubt that the major foreign-owned or foreign-based firms (the French and Japanese importers, Vauxhall-Opel and Ford of Europe) would prefer to import all of their sales to Britain. In that way they could capture even greater returns between the lower unit cost of production elsewhere in Europe and the extremely high level of retail prices for cars in Britain. But to attempt this would be to court further import controls. The case of the UK is worth pursuing in this respect since it shows the extent of the cost penalty which is imposed upon car manufacturers, and,

1. "Pacts for Motor Industries Urged", *F.T.*, 28:4:82.
2. "Labour call for ban on foreign car sales in UK", *F.T.*, 1:5:80.
3. "Nissen to resist plant conditions", *F.T.*, 25:9:81.
4. "Nissan promises to build cars more British than the British", *The Economist*, 5:12:81.
5. "Detroit, Argentina", *Wall Street Journal*, 28:4:82.

TABLE 8.4

UK MOTOR VEHICLE PRODUCTION, MONTHLY AVERAGE, 1946-1981,
(Units: '000s)

	Total	of which: for export	Exports as % of output
1946	18.3	8.3	45
1947	23.9	12.9	54
1948	27.9	19.7	71
1949	34.4	22.7	66
1950	43.5	34.1	78
1951	39.7	30.6	77
1952	37.3	22.9	61
1953	49.6	26.1	53
1954	64.1	33.2	52
1955	74.8	32.6	44
1956	59.0	29.7	50
1957	71.7	38.5	54
1958	87.6	43.5	50
1959	99.2	50.9	51
1960	112.7	47.9	43
1961	83.7	33.5	40
1962	104.1	45.9	44
1963	134.0	54.1	40
1964	155.6	58.8	38
1965	143.5	54.4	38
1966	133.6	52.1	39
1967	129.3	47.0	36
1968	151.3	66.9	44
1969	143.1	68.7	48
1970	136.7	60.2	44
1971	145.2	59.5	41
1972	160.1	51.1	32
1973	145.6	50.4	35
1974	127.8	49.7	39
1975	105.6	44.3	42
1976	111.1	47.1	42
1977	109.7	46.9	43
1978	101.9	41.2	40
1979	89.2	32.7	37
1980	77.0	29.1	38
1981	79.6	25.4	32

SOURCE : CSO 'Economic Trends' 1982

by implication, their customers, by governments' interference in optimal location decisions.

Table 8.4 shows the rise and fall of British car production since the second world war. From a level of 18,300 per month in 1946, output grew to a peak at 160,000 per month in 1972 and then fell back, reaching an average of 78,300 per month during 1980 and 1981. Output in the last three years has thus receded to its levels of the late 1950s. Export sales have similarly declined, although some evasion of the very high export share seen in the 1940s was inevitable, given the manifest recovery of the car industry elsewhere in Europe and its emergence in certain developing countries.

A study which goes a long way to explaining the vast gap which built up in the UK between sales and domestic output is that produced by Ford of Europe in 1981. Establishing that identical Escort models cost $1,000 each more to produce at Halewood, England than at Saarlouis, West Germany despite a $5.25 per hour lower wage in England. Ford's study identified major productivity differences between the two plants. Man-hours per car at Saarlouis (at 21) were almost half the 40 needed at Halewood[1]. Commenting on the major BL strike of late 1981, a financial correspondent interpreted the problem thus: "Because Britain is a bad place to make cars, to retain that industrial function makes extraordinary demands on the labour force, demands that it very naturally will resist ... the workforce (may have) taken the decision that the sacrifice needed from them for Britain to continue as a fairly independent producer of volume cars is not acceptable[2]." The point at principle here is that, in any economy, there is an hourly wage which, in combination with a given level of hourly output, will make production profitable and marketable. Above that wage, however, continued production, with unchanged productivity is clearly only enforceable through trade barriers, or through administrative action, such as employment subsidies, to offset costs.

III Will tastes converge?

Judging the extent to which consumers' preferences in car design and characteristics may in future evolve is obviously a hazardous business. An initial point to be made is that the importance of tastes convergence is a question of extent. Clearly, it is not an imperative for the world car concept that consumers all over the world should want to buy identical cars. For one thing, governments have already negated that possibility by applying divergent standards on such factors as fuel emissions and safety. Moreover, the physical characteristics of countries differ, and will to some degree also be reflected in consumers' preferences. But the point remains that there must be sufficient homogeneity of tastes internationally for a small number (probably below five) of floor-pan designs to be acceptable worldwide. If this portfolio of choices is not

---

1. "Ford UK and German plants offer a study in contrasts", *Herald Tribune,* 15:10:81.
2. Financial Leader, *The Guardian,* 3:11:81.

sufficient to capture what a large proportion of the car-buying public wants, the arguments over economies of scale fall to the ground.

Most commentators would nonetheless accept that a very basic degree of international inter-changeability is likely to succeed. The sort of differences in taste seen between developing country markets have tended so far to be matters of emphasis more than anything else. For instance, Ford of Europe obviously sells the same basic cars throughout Europe, and merely differentiates minor factors such as relatively sombre features for the British fleet buyer but more exhuberant styling for French personal buyers[1].

Already, too, widespread inter-changeability of components ("inter-model commonality") is established practice. In this context too, therefore, the future use of world components is a question of extent rather than principle.

Given these observations, what is the extent of this commitment to world cars and world components?

IV   Whither the world car?

Enough has been said here about the world car concept to demonstrate that it is unlikely ever to be a significant *modus operandi* in the more simple terms in which it was once described. There are too many factors militating against the internationalization of production in the 1980s to allow the concept — however attractive its intrinsic merits may be — to reach full fruition. But this is not to say that nothing will come of it. Already it is plain that the interchange of parts between, for example, the USA and Mexico is bound to grow very substantially. The increased resort, on the part of Japanese firms, to joint ventures in more and more developing countries, again using a certain commonality of components, looks equally assured. What is, then, likely to evolve among the world's car manufacturers is a commitment to some of the elements of the world car concept. The extent and the degree of that commitment is likely to differ considerably between manufacturers and, by virtue of international trade regulations, between countries where manufacturers are located. There may well also be some form of life cycle at work within the world car, such that firms at different stages of development and maturity differ in the degree of their involvement in the world car. This section elucidates these ideas.

As the biggest single source of cars in the world, it is appropriate to begin by looking at the future of the world car in Japan.

The Japanese firms' commitment to the world car is likely to be the least among all developed country-based manufacturers. The conventional mix of home

---

1.   "West Germany: Ford makes a U-turn back into profits lane." *Business Week,* 12:4:82.

production, modified for developing countries by joint ventures where appropriate, is likely to remain the preferred form. True internationalization of production is not at all the path these firms identify as being in their best interest. Why?

First, it is clear that cost conditions alone allow the Japanese firms very great worldwide competitive advantage. To quote figures used in a recent study of the car industry[1], car output per employee in Japan in 1978 was 16.3 per year. In the US the equivalent figure was 20.9 (adjusted for size differences) while in the UK the output was only 4.7; in Germany 8.6; in France, 6.6; and in Italy, 6.2. Since 1978, however, there is reason to believe that Japanese productivity improvements have opened up a very major gap over the US level. By late 1981, estimates being circulated in the US firms, drawing on the work of Professor Abernathy of Harvard Business School and of James Harbour and Associates, pointed to a 2:1 differential in favour of Japan. Harbour and Associates estimate that 14 man-hours of assembly work are used on a Japanese-built car as against 29 in the US industry. Attaching a labour cost per hour of $19 in the US, and $12.50 in Japan, the Japanese firms had established on labour cost grounds alone a unit cost differential of $1,600-$1,700[2]. This would be somewhat offset by the $450/car cost of shipping the products across the Pacific to the USA, but, after factoring in capital cost and non-labour material input costs, the Japanese firms still enjoy a unit cost advantage of $1,500-$2,000.

What is important about these cost figures is not just the absolute advantage they indicate that the Japanese possess — critically important though it obviously is — but also the extent to which it may be replicated across a number of locations. Identifying the sources of Japanese cost advantage according to the stage of manufacture at which they arise allows one to assess how far the Japanese advantage may be "exported", and with it the beginnings of Japanese-based international production networks. The overwhelming source of the cost differential — labour productivity — has already been mentioned. While hourly labour rates would be still lower in developing country locations, the very tight quality control which goes with it in Japan may well not be so readily transferable. What is important in Japanese factories is the orientation of each small work-group to rigorous quality control at each stage of production, not just at the final stage of inspection. Harbour and Associates estimate that Japanese quality controls save $184 per car, as a result of less scrappage and reworking, fewer warranty claims and fewer inspectors being needed. The entire system is based on "defect prevention", in Harbour's words. There is evidence that industrial relations can be improved noticeably by applying Japanese-style management patterns in other countries (among Japanese-run plants in the UK, for

---

1. D.T.Jones, "Maturity and Crisis in the European Car Industry", (Sussex European Papers, no.8, Sussex University, 1981).
2. "Can Detroit ever come back?" *US News & World Report,* 8:3:82;
    "Autos: Studying the Japanese", *New York Times,* 27:2:82;
    "Can Detroit Catch Up?" *Fortune,* 8:2:82;
    W.J.Abernathy, *The Productivity Dilemma: Roadblock to Innovation in the Automobile Industry,* (Johns Hopkins Press, 1978).

instance, the incidence of strikes is much less than in British-run plants). But the quality control procedures and attitudes, tightly embedded as they are in social practices, are unlikely to be so replicable elsewhere. Indeed, after studying US and Japanese car plants in considerable detail Abernathy and Clark of Harvard Business School doubted that mere tinkering with innovations such as quality circles would suffice; what was necessary was "getting the whole workforce-management picture straightened out"[1]. The reluctance of Honda and Nissan to recognize United Auto Workers' organising in their new plants also reflects deep Japanese concern about traditional US labour practices[2].

Manufacture abroad would, on the other hand, yield a smaller shipping charge. But this would be balanced by the loss of the extremely tight inventory control system (known as the "just in time" system) used in Japanese car plants. Relying on many feeder firms, for up to 70% of the value of the finished car, Japanese factories allow for very little inventory to be carried. US car firms are estimated by Harbour and Associates to carry $775-worth of stocks and work in progress for each car they produce, whereas in Japan the figure is closer to $150. There are corresponding savings on plants' floor area, heating and stock management. Using some of the Japanese approach, Chrysler in the US has cut from $2 billion to $600 million the value of the parts inventory it carries at any given time. In 1982 GM was estimated to be paying $3 billion annually to service its $9 billion-worth of inventory: a struggle to cut this bill by 60% is now underway[3]. Once again, however, what matters is that if production or assembly were transferred more and more to overseas locations, this tight stock control system would be jeopardised and costs would rise accordingly. On this point another management consultancy is firm: "A lot of Toyota's advantage is not directly transferable" was a comment made on the inventory-control advantages witnessed in the plant at Toyota City[4]. Moreover, studies commissioned by Toyota itself on the feasibility of a US operation, concluded that the risks were too high. The firm believes it can raise its share of world sales from 8.4% in 1981 to 10% by 1985 without US production[5]. Chief of Fiat, Gianni Agnelli, has confirmed that the Japanese advantage would be eroded in Europe: "their manufacturing in Europe would face the same problems we do"[6].

The evidence seems to point to the Japanese firms being reluctant to transfer production overseas to any significant extent. Faced with the threat of growing import restrictions, however, they have to respond in some way. The evidence available to date suggests that their reaction will differ according to the country in question. In developing countries, the least disadvantageous outcome for Japanese firms is the joint venture. This has the advantage of at least affording access to the market

---

1. "Economists offer advice to American automakers", *Automotive News,* 15:2:82.
2. "Honda ends opposition to auto union's efforts", *New York Times,* 23:4:82.
3. "Automakers have trouble with 'Kanban'", *Wall Street Journal,* 7:4:82.
4. "The Company that stopped Detroit", *New York Times,* 21:3:82.
5. "Why Toyota feels it can afford to go it alone", *F.T.,* 24:8:81.
6. "Fiat's view of the world", *Autocar,* 15:5:82.

in question — and, as earlier chapters have indicated, it is the developing country markets which will yield the fastest growth henceforth. Given that virtually no developing country government now allows unlimited access for fully-assembled cars, and furthermore insists upon exacting various local content regulations to benefit domestic parts suppliers, this is clearly the best of a sub-optimal set of choices. Even Toyota had 11 plants overseas by late 1981, while, in Asian developing countries alone, Nissan possesses 8; Honda, 7; Toyo Kogyo, 6; Mitsubishi, 3; Isusu, 3; and Suzuki, 1. Across Indonesia, the Philippines, Thailand, South Korea, Malaysia, Singapore, Pakistan and Iran seven Japanese car firms between them owned 38 assembly plants by 1980.

An illustration of this in practice is the 1982 joint venture agreement between Maruti, India's moribund state-owned car firm, and Suzuki. A short-list of three firms (Suzuki, Nissan and Mitsubishi) was selected from an international competition attracting BL, Renault and others[1]. The Indian Public Investment Board selected Suzuki, which agreed to invest $300 million in India's first big private foreign investment deal in over ten years. By 1988 annual output should have grown to 100,000, well beyond the 31,000 output level achieved in 1981 by the two totally-protected Indian firms Hindusthan Motors of Calcutta and Premier Automobiles of Bombay. Relaxations on the importation of certain components have been guaranteed; this will be essential given the unsuitability of many Indian engineering items for the Japanese cars[2]. Although Suzuki is understood to have agreed in principle to export some of its output through its own marketing network, it is unlikely that these exports will ever amount to much. The Indian authorities are, naturally, keen to maximise the foreign exchange benefits of the Suzuki presence — the more so if the proportion of imported components is to be high — but quality may not be sufficient. Even exporting to nearby Pakistan appears to have been foreclosed by a prior agreement, again with Suzuki, to begin local assembly there.

In developing country locations, then, the advantage of having relatively privileged access to a controlled market appears to outweigh the disadvantage of not being able to run a plant as rigorously as in Japan itself. The same point applies to US and European-based firms too. In developed country locations, however, by virtue of the characteristics of their manufacturing process as described earlier, the Japanese-based firms are far more wary about relocating than are other developed country firms. An illustration of a preferred strategy for the Japanese is provided by the recent GM-Toyota talks.

Early in 1982 it was confirmed that joint production of small cars in the USA might ensue, with GM gaining from Toyota's expertise in sub-compact manufacture. Already GM is planning that its next small car should be built in conjunction with its Japanese affiliates Isuzu (of which it own 34.2%) and Suzuki (5.3%)[3]. Toyota would

---

1. "Japanese car groups fill Maruti partner shortlist", *F.T.*, 31:3:82.
2. "India puts Japan behind the wheel", *The Economist*, 24:4:82.
3. "GM, Toyota discuss venture to make small cars in US", *Herald Tribune*, 9:3:82.

gain more secure long-term access to the US market. For Toyota, the venture would offer a relatively low-risk entrée to the US, not jeopardizing its own quality-control reputation[1]. Table 8.1 indicates that wherever possible Japanese firms source a far higher share of their cars outside the US than do, say, VW.

TABLE 8.5

EXTENT OF FOREIGN SOURCING BY CAR FIRMS WITH US ASSEMBLY FACILITIES, 1982

Firm	Facility	Foreign sourcing (%)
(a) **Non-US firms**		
VW of America Inc.	New Stanton, Pa.	30%
Honda of America	Marysville, Ohio	60%
Nissan USA	Smyrna, Tenn.	68%
(b) **US firms**		
American Motors	Kenosha, Wi.	
	(Renault R9 plant)	33%
Ford Motor Co.	All plants together	94%
GM	All plants together	n.a.
Chrysler Corp.	All plants together	95%

Source: "Sourcing, The Automakers", *Ward's Auto World,* May 1982

An agreement which is similar in principle is that between Nissan and VW, only that one entails VW gaining more access to the Japanese domestic market by joint production, by 1988, of up to 120-200,000 units annually with Japan[2]. At present VW, while the biggest importer to Japan, sells only 20,000 units per year. All imports in 1981 totalled 38.110 units, or 0.7% of the market[3]. Some 80% of the proposed VW-Nissan cars would be sold in Japan and the balance exported.

What other European car firms fear most about the VW-Nissan agreement is, of course, that it might be put into reverse and used as an entrée for Nissan for further

---

1. "Toyota and GM: Shadow-Boxing", *The Economist,* 17:3:82.
2. "A bid to pull down import barriers", *F.T.,* 4:12:80.
3. "Ford, VW Changing Gears in Japan", *Wall Street Journal,* 15:1:82.

exports in Europe. (The reactions within Europe to the BL-Honda agreement are discussed earlier in this chapter.) Similar objections to unrestricted imports from Spain may attend VW's proposed manufacture of cars, under licence, in Spain. Some 130,000 units per year might be produced in association with SEAT after 1984[1]. At present VW sells only 3,000 cars annually in Spain, and although Spanish sales would be the primary objective further exports to supplement German output would be part of the plan.

Once again, however, the Japanese firms' strategy must be tailored to reality. Already Honda is committed to producing cars at a plant in Ohio from November 1982, while Nissan will begin to build light pick-up trucks in Tennessee, in 1983. Given the economic and political factors which, as in developing country locations, make US factories the best from a sub-optimal portfolio of choices, the Japanese firms do attempt to make the most of their public relations opportunities. In an annual PR report, Toyota records that in 1981 its 32,000 American employees earned $614 million[2].

Turning now to US-based firms, what form of world cars will they evolve? The first clearcut world car is, as has been noted already, the GM J-car, which will be produced in eight locations, and with five nameplates in the USA. Production locations are the USA, Canada, West Germany, Belgium, the UK, Japan, South Africa, Australia and Brazil. By late 1982 four plants in the US were devoted to J-car production. All the established divisions, Cadillac, Buick, Chevrolet, Oldsmobile and Pontiac, have a version of the J-car. So do Opel, Vauxhall, GM-Holden in Australia and the affiliates elsewhere, as Chart 7 shows.

What inferences can be drawn from this for other world car projects based in the US? First, it is plain that even the J-car is not fully a world car insofar as its components are not fully interchangeable: "not one single component (apart from nuts and bolts) will fit J-cars made in North America and those made elsewhere. With the J-car GM had to go for compatibility rather than commonality of components[3]." Second, the difficulty in gaining acceptance of a design among buyers in many different countries of the world at the same time has told. Thus differences of design do persist between the production locations, with the US cars more elaborately fitted. This level of differentiation by market was, however, always anticipated, as is consistent with the plans for the car. Further evidence of distinct differences in taste persisting comes from the fact that GM has dropped plans to make the new small car (the S-car) a world car in the full sense. It will simply be too small for the USA. And in any case, as has already been noted, it is by no means clear that US firms have yet evinced any particular flair for building very small cars. Otherwise, why would they be discussing co-production with various Japanese firms?

---

1. "VW and SEAT discuss licensing", *F.T.*, 4:5:82.
2. "Japanese auto makers raise the red, white and blue", *Detroit News,* 14:4:82.
3. "The J-car: GM's global jigsaw", *F.T.*, 26:8:81.

CHART 7

GM PUTTING THE WORLD CAR TOGETHER

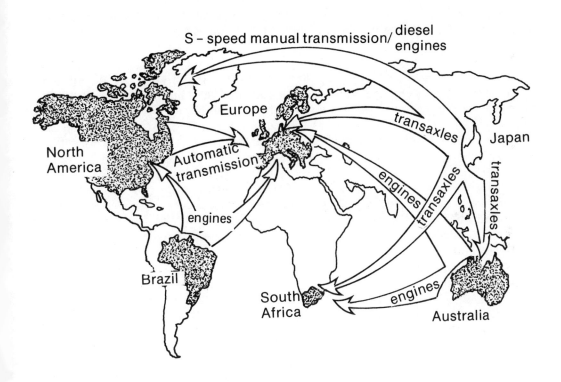

Data on the extent of overseas sourcing for cars to be sold in the US by US-based firms has in the past confirmed that US firms prefer local inputs. Figures for the 1970s showed very clearly that "international sourcing in low-wage developing countries for use by parent companies in their home markets is insignificant. Such countries are also unimportant as suppliers of subsidiaries in third regions[1]". Recently, parts from Mexico have become more significant, however, with not just US firms, but French, German and Japanese firms involved. By 1984, a survey suggested that 1.7 million engines per year would be made in Mexico and sent to the US. These will be worth $500 million annually, as against their 1981 value of $50 million[2]. With wage costs in northern Mexico averaging $2.15 per hour, and the need, imposed by the Mexican government, to have countervailing finance to offset the cost of importing fully-assembled cars from the US, this inter-change is likely to become very important. Indeed, drawing upon this pattern, the president of Ford has argued that this is the type of interchange that will increasingly characterize the world car: "I think world trade in built-up vehicles will be largely replaced by trade in vehicle components ... The distinction between imports and domestics could very well become meaningless[3]".

For Europe the nature of the world car is likely to be different again. This stems largely from the fact that as accustomed large-scale car exporters for the best part of the post-war period, now seeing many of their non-European overseas market shut by restrictions, overseas assembly is the natural response. But, as has been seen, assembly within, say, Nigeria, exclusively for sales there, is not a true application of the world car concept.

The involvement of European firms in US assembly has a chequered history. After first following Ford and GM into a European acquisition (rather too late, as it turned out, and with a poor choice) Chrysler found itself in 1978 having those operations being taken over by Peugeot-Citroen. This was merely part of a process whereby Chrysler entered the 1970s with subsidiaries in 26 countries and left the 1970s in bankruptcy. The 1978 agreement involved $300 million in cash being transferred to Chrysler in the US, and a 15% stake in Chrysler taken by Peugeot. At the same time the Argentine offshoot was acquired by VW, who also took a majority stake in Chrysler's Brazilian subsidiary. Mitsubishi took 30% of Chrysler's Australian firm; South African entrepreneurs took 75% of the South African firm[4].

VW has had considerable success with its first US plant in Pennsylvania, which began operating in April 1978. With VW Rabbit models with 25% local content being produced initially, local content rose to 75% by late 1979. Unlike the threat of import controls, the VW direct investment decision was largely prompted by the drift of costs. By 1976 VW had seen its US sales fall from their 1970 peak share of 7.2% to

1. G.Maxcy, op.cit.
2. "US imports Mexican car engines", *Journal of Commerce,* 12:4:82.
3. Donald Peterson quoted in "World Car", *I.H.T.,* Sept.1981 supplement on cars.
4. G.Maxcy, *The Multinational Motor Industry,* (London, Croom Helm, 1981).

only 2.1%. This threatened the firm's dealer network and made imperative a decision to start domestic assembly.

Production from a second US plant has been indefinitely postponed. The Sterling Heights, Detroit, site was to start producing in 1982 but the losses sustained in 1980 by VW in the US (DM 90 million) and the slide in worldwide profits, from DM 667 million in 1979 to DM 136 million in 1981, have, in conjunction with depressed US sales overall, altered the outlook. 1981 VW sales in the US fell 37% to 53,000, reflecting the overall bad climate for small cars that year, and in May 1982 the daily production schedule was cut from 846/day to 724.

European firms' involvement in non-US overseas operations is also a mixed history. While some ventures have been successes, others have turned sour. As is the case at many junctures of business, the problem posed in the latter cases is to judge the extent to which improvement in the economic environment is sufficient to restore the operation to health.

A particular difficulty of this sort has faced VW's South American operations in the recent past. Mounting economic problems (most obviously, soaring inflation and an unsustainably large current account deficit) forced the Brazilian government into a major austerity plan, the main victim of which, in 1981 and 1982, was the car industry. Car sales in 1981 were down 40% on 1980, and in an 800,000-1 million per year market that type of drop obviously pushes unit costs up very sharply indeed. VW in Brazil lost $50 million in 1981, but to protect the longterm interests of this subsidiary (80% VW-owned) the parent firm injected $80 million of new equity. Similarly in Argentina, economic difficulties have made serious inroads into European firms' prospects. VW injected $45 million into its Argentinian subsidiary late in 1981, in the face of a 30% sales drop. In the first quarter of 1982 sales there were at their lowest for 16 years[1]. So bad was the position for Peugeot that it closed its Argentinian operation completely, with consequent write-off costs estimated at $250 million[2].

Overall, VW is apparently resigned to the idea that the bulk of its sales growth in the 1980s must come from outside Germany. The DM 13 billion worldwide investment scheme for 1981-83 concentrates on overseas operation, although already in the 1972-80 period the firm's overseas output has almost doubled to 1.1 million units[3].

V Escape up-market?

Much of the discussion about the world car from within the industry itself implies that the objective of the restructuring it requires is an attempt to meet head-on the

---

1. "South American car industry", *The Economist,* 10:4:82.
2. "Peugeot blames Argentine closure for high deficit", *F.T.,* 29:4:82.
3. "VW and the parable of the fat runner", *F.T.,* 30:4:82.

Japanese challenge. The fundamental path of thinking which underlies this point of view is that the emergence of the Japanese firms after the mid-1980s as major world-wide competitors, whose price and cost levels lay substantially below those pertaining in the older-established firms in the west, changed irreversibly the level of competition in the whole industry. To come anywhere near to matching the Japanese cost levels, therefore, it was essential to restructure US and European manufacturing operations. But another strategy does suggest itself — one of relinquishing, over a period of time, the market for small and relatively cheap cars to the Japanese firms, and concentrating on the upper segments of car demand where most of the US tradition and experience lies. The immediate attraction of this approach is that it emphasises the larger-bodied car, the product from which the US-based firms have traditionally made the bulk of their profits. What might the prospects for such a strategy be?

On the surface, there would appear to be one overwhelming attraction in the strategy — the proven loyalty of the US consumer to the large-bodied car.

On the other hand, there are two very substantial difficulties involved in this strategy. First, and ironically, as a direct consequence of the volume controls placed upon the number of cars they can export to the USA and most of Europe, Japanese firms are, quite rationally, altering the mix of cars they offer abroad. This allows them, by offering larger and more expensive models, to increase the unit revenue they obtain, partially to compensate themselves for the fact that their volumes are frozen for the foreseeable future. Clearly, it is preferable to sell 10,000 cars at $10,000 each than 10,000 cars at $8,000. In doing this, Japanese car producers are simply following what has been done in other industries, for instance, textiles and clothing, whenever the volume of imports allowed into a country has been frozen. The unintended consequence for the US domestic producers, however, is that they now face competition on large cars as well as compacts. Moreover, to the extent that the Japanese firms judge the total market open to them (in the US this means 1.68 million plus 16.5% of any market growth over 1981's 8.5 million unit level) worth fighting over, one would expect to see attempts at trade diversion between firms. As Toyota and Honda fight for greater market share within their alloted ceiling, price competition must eventually intensify, and leave the US firms' products even more exposed on price terms. There is certainly evidence of vigorous price competition between Japanese firms within Japan: Toyota and Nissan, with 38% and 29% respectively of the 1981 market, are aggressively pursuing the 3.2 million car market foreseen for 1982[1].

Evidence that car importers to the US in general (not just the Japanese, who in the last three years have been accounting for three-quarters of all US imports) are already moving upstream comes from Chart 8, which shows that by 1981 imported cars were in fact selling, on a weighted average basis, at more than US-built cars. This is a clear signal that the importing firms have the correct marketing image to allow them to charge more for their products if they so choose. Evidence also comes from recent model introductions from many Japanese firms. Notable is Mitsubishi,

---

1. "Japanese cars: traffic jam", *The Economist*, 13:2:82.

CHART 8

PRICE SWITCH — AVERAGE CAR PRICES

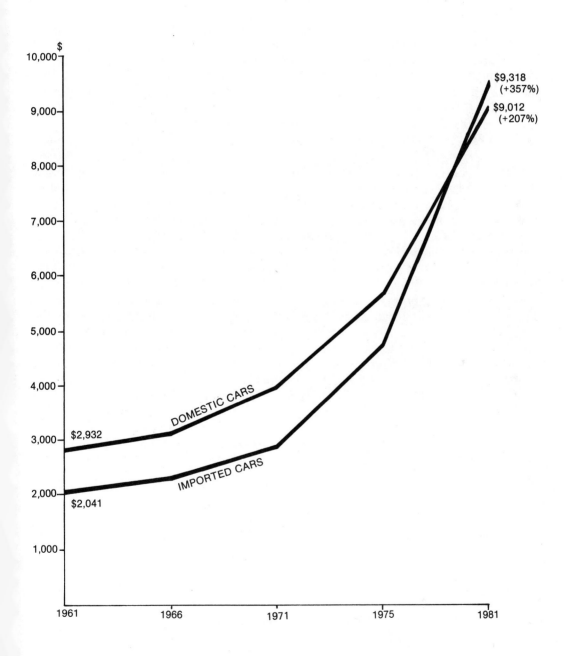

whose cars have been sold through Chrysler dealers in volumes averaging 170,000 annually since 1980. 1982 saw much higher prices (in excess of $11,000) being exacted for more luxurious cars: "Mitsubishi's shrewd strategy to wring the most revenue out of a restricted market[1]". Nissan, too, is acknowledged already to be considering "broadening its US line to include mid-sized models crammed with electronics[2]".

Similar remarks apply to Europe too. In 1981 it was announced that, following the success of the BL-Honda co-operation with the small saloon (known in Britain as the Acclaim) a large executive car would also be co-produced. Being a comparative latecomer to the car business (having started in motorcycles) Honda was keen to gain UK experience with larger designs[3]. The XX project, as it is known, reflects Honda's desire to expand beyond small and medium-sized cars for export, while Honda will also sell the XX through the BL marketing network in Japan itself[4]. Production should start in 1985.

The second reason for doubting that the Japanese challenge, in the US market at least, can be in part resolved by a change in product emphasis on the part of US firms, is that prices must be seen by consumers to move together. Once again, the clear inference of the last three years' sales figures in the USA is that if small-sized cars are felt to be too expensive relative to larger cars the former will meet stiff consumer resistance. Given this, the reverse must almost certainly be the case too — even bearing in mind the US predilection, other things being equal, for a large-sized car. The 1980 Cadillac Seville, for instance, retailed at around $22,000 and was quite simply felt to be overpriced, irrespective of its merits. Similarly with the 1982 GM J-cars, which were introduced onto a depressed market and a flat economy at premium prices of up to $12,200 — well over the price that outside observers expected[5]. What is at stake here is not so much the intrinsic merit of a car but its perceived value to the public. And, as manufacturers have often found to their cost since 1979, the price and the physical characteristics of the car must, in some indefinable way, appear suited to one another. Thus, there would appear to be no easy escape-route back to enhanced profitability through a strategy of premium-priced full-sized cars coupled with abandoning the lower-priced segments to the Japanese. For the car market operates as a whole, even though an individual's purchase is only from within a small segment of that whole.

---

1. "Mitsubishi revs up to go solo", *Business Week,* 3:5:82.
2. "Japan's automakers shift strategies", *Fortune,* 11:8:80.
3. "BL-Honda: Success at high speed", *F.T.,* 8:12:81.
4. "How Honda sees BL", *F.T.* 13:11:81.
5. "GM's J-car campaign hits snags", *Herald Tribune,* 27:4:82.

Chapter Nine

Conclusions: The World Car Compromise

In conclusion, it can be seen that there exists a fairly wide degree of consensus among car industry commentators over a number of issues. In particular, the slowing down in the pace at which car sales in the more mature markets in North America and Western Europe grow is almost universally expected. Similarly with the much faster growth of sales in the relatively unmotorised countries of the third world. Given the enormous disparity in absolute market size, however, there will clearly still be a great deal of business to be done in the mature markets — the more so if more ambitious and luxurious models can be sold in preference to more basic models. The markets in some of the developing countries will, however, be circumscribed to some degree by political uncertainties and, in the case of countries where importing of fully-assembled cars continues, by periodic import freezes in response to balance of payments crises.

The factors on which there is far less agreement concern the patterns of international investment, production and trade which may evolve in the 1980s. Towards the late 1970s there was growing up a new view about the car industry's prospects which became virtually the new orthodoxy. This argued that because the industry had suddenly become more competitive (presumably, although this was not always made explicit, due to the arrival of aggressive Japanese producers) far greater use of economies of scale would have to be made. This in turn required that smaller firms should amalgamate, or at least co-operate, or go out of business. Thus the 1980s would witness, in the words of Lee Iococca, President of Chrysler, a "third industrial revolution" in which a great shake-out of firms would take place. Only a few giants, such as Datsun, General Motors and Renault-plus-Peugeot, would survive, according to this view. Once assembled, these giant firms would then integrate their assembly and manufacturing networks so as to build and sell at will across the world, minimising cost and maximising revenue, while offering an essentially similar range of models across the world. Brazilian workers would build engines for American consumers' small cars; Spanish consumers would buy cars designed by Germans in Detroit and assembled by Portuguese from components manufactured over three continents.

A great deal of the evidence put together in this study serves to question this thinking. It may not be entirely wrong. But it is unlikely to be entirely right. It is a question of extent. While the evidence does point to a greater degree of price competition in the early 1980s, there are no obvious reasons for doubting that small-scale producers can coexist alongside giant firms. Indeed, in recent years some of the smaller firms like BMW, Mercedes and Porsche have been among the most spectacularly successful in the whole industry. Small can be profitable. Nor is there any unambiguous evidence of growing similarity in tastes across the world, of sufficient extent to allow firms to make broadly similar offerings in a variety of different countries. Certainly the behaviour of American car buyers in the last three or four years has been obstinately American and un-European: full-sized cars have sold in surprisingly large volumes and some new European-styled models, for all their fuel economy, have been shunned. It remains to be seen how consumers in the middle-income developing countries will wish their cars to look and perform. Most evidence so far points to Japanese-based models, and certain simpler European designs, such as the VW Beetle, being very popular.

Finally, there is the question of how possible it will still be to ship cars at will across borders in the years to come. Governments have tended to be involved in the car industry to a great degree; with trade policy and industrial policy so much to the fore in politicians' thinking at present it would be hazardous to imagine that they will willingly see their power over these crucial issues taken away or undercut by a further round of internationalization in the car industry. While it is true that car firms employ under 7% of the manufacturing labour-force in European countries (although considerably more in the USA) a car plant tends to be big. It is also usually politically visible. For these reasons considerable pressure has always been placed upon politicians to circumvent employers' closure decisions whenever possible. Employment subsidies or even outright nationalization tend to be undertaken instead.

There are, then, a number of barriers in the way of the ultra-competitive, truly multinational, car industry that has been envisaged by some writers. Nationalism is perhaps the most intransigent problem here. Referring to a proposed Japanese plan to ship Australian-assembled Mitsubishi cars into the UK, a dealer who saw his own sales threatened said: "It does not matter whether the cars come from Australia or Timbuktu, the cars are still Japanese." This line, for all its costs for car buyers, and frustrations for cost-conscious production planners, is likely to hold sway so long as unemployment in the West stays high and productivity differentials stay wide. The new age of the truly stateless car, like the classless society, seems as far away as ever.

The outlook for sales to 1985

It is clear from the accompanying tables of new car registrations that 1981 and 1982 were generally disappointing years for the automobile industry. In 1981 new car sales in the USA, at 8.53 million units were lower than at any time since 1975. Domestically-made car sales, at 6.24 million, were the worst since 1961. And this followed 1980, itself by no means a good year. Moreover, 1982 was scarcely any improvement; in the first six months of the year, US new car registrations were a further 9.9 per cent lower than in the comparable period of 1981. Elsewhere, there were poor sales too. And there was increasing pressure, documented elsewhere in this study, for imports to be restricted from many markets so that domestic producers could at least obtain a higher share of what few sales were to be gained. Some particularly poor sales were also recorded outside the car industry's main centres. In Brazil and Argentina, for instance, two of the major developing country markets, sales and production plunged in 1982. A strong contrast was South Africa, where even the record sales level of 1981 was being exceeded in the first four months of 1982.

How long will it be until the car producers can look forward once more to growing sales? This section examines the constraints and some of the positive factors at work in the market at present and likely to be important until 1985.

The main obstacles facing a resumption of growth in the developed countries' car markets derive from the persistence of the recession which dates from 1980. But recessions are virtually inevitably accompanied by weak sales for consumer durables such as cars. So what more specific factors can be identified as being at work, and when might they change?

The central point about recessions for car purchase is that they typically result in falling real disposable income for households. This is for various reasons: bankruptcies and lay-offs cut the number of people in work; less overtime is worked; and the scope for pay rises in excess of price rises, to boost real income, is diminished as competition between firms for shrinking markets is intensified. This means that the amount of money available for committing to major new durables purchases is no longer rising at the accustomed trend rate. Indeed, real income may be falling for some households in some countries. In the UK, for instance, although real post-tax household income actually increased (by 1.1 per cent) in 1980 despite the onset of the recession — surprising car producers who had expected a much worse year — in 1981 it fell by 2.0 per cent and in the early part of 1982 was still falling. By that stage it was back to its 1978 level.

Another factor which may be at work in recessions — and which is unmistakeably present in the current recession — is a tendency for households to save an abnormally high proportion of their income. This tendency has been growing for the last decade but is still not fully understood by economists. Two theories which may be operating at present are first that when unemployment is very high people save a higher proportion of their earnings than usual as a precautionary measure, and second that their savings are high simply because interest-rates are high. For the last three years most industrialized countries have certainly seen high interest-rates (even when adjusted for price rises) and have seen unemployment growing steadily. In many countries savings have been unexpectedly high too. This means that durables purchases are squeezed even further, since a smaller proportion even of the smaller incomes being earned in a recession is allocated to spending. There is, finally, a further relationship between high interest-rates and car purchases in that high interest rates naturally imply more costly monthly housing loan repayments. This in turn means less is available for spending on other goods and services.

In addition to these depressive factors being at work the second-hand car market has been depressed in many countries. The consequence of this is to reduce the trade-in value of the cars already owned, widening the gap which has to be bridged by a new loan or cash payment. While it is true that rebates and special offers have effectively cut the retail price of new cars too, the gap is apparently proving unbridgeable for many consumers at present.

Two factors weigh against these points. First is the fact that all the time a lot of households are deferring replacement of their cars the overall age of the stock of cars held in the country is rising. There are limits, set by precedent and by the physical longevity of cars, to how long this deferring of purchases can go on. Eventually there will be a reaction. The second point about the car market which needs to be borne in mind is that it does not always conform to the type of rational analysis just set out. In Italy in 1980 and 1981, for instance, manufacturers were continually being surprised by the strength of the market. At a time when the country's economic situation was becoming quite serious (particularly towards the end of 1980) new car sales continued to plough ahead of all forecasts. It may have been that the black or underground economy was still generating income from which people could draw in order to buy new cars. One can never verify this possibility. Or — another interpretation put forward — the jump in the cost of housing during this period discouraged prospective home-owners who used accumulated savings to buy a new car instead of a new house. The fact that even after the event one cannot establish with certainty the truth of these theories means that there will remain a capricious and unpredictable element to all car sales forecasts.

Looking beyond 1982, 1983 appears likely to be a year of modest recovery from the 1980-82 recession. In its July 1982 *Economic Outlook* the OECD forecast that the developed countries' GNP should rise by only 0.5 per cent in 1982 but by around 2.5 per cent in 1983. In the US, GNP should rise by about 2 per cent in 1983 after actually falling (by some 1.5 per cent) in 1982, whereas in Europe a recovery from 1.5 per cent GDP growth in 1982 to 2.5 per cent growth in 1983 is foreseen. For the US economy, real disposable income, after rising by an estimated 2.2 per cent in 1981 and 2.0 per cent in 1982, is expected to grow by 3 per cent in 1983. Private spending is however expected to grow a little less than this — by 1.5 per cent in 1982 and 2.8 per cent in 1983. Furthermore, outlays involving credit extensions are expected to remain particularly subdued. As the OECD secretariat put it:

> "Persistently high real interest and unemployment rates are expected to hold consumer credit extensions at substantially lower levels than in the last few years, making the rebound of consumers' expenditure moderate by historic standards, even interrupting it in the first half of 1983 when fiscal stimuli abate."[1]

Despite this relatively slow recovery, 1983 may nonetheless witness a recovery of the new car market to its 1979 level. This would mean sales of 10.3 million units. The share of imports within total sales is an important point for the US producers. 1980 saw imports accounting for 28.2 per cent of US new car sales. Within this total

---

1. OECD, *Economic Outlook,* July 1982 issue (Paris: OECD, 1982).

Japanese producers took around 20 per cent. The imposition of the "voluntary export restraint" by the US on Japanese producers means that they will be held to a share of 19.6 per cent of the 1981 market plus per cent of any increment occurring subsequently. In a 10.3 million unit market this would restrict Japanese sales to 1.97 million units.

For the European market, a recovery of similar magnitude in 1983 might lead to 10.7 million cars being sold. This would represent a 700,000 unit or 7 per cent improvement over 1982.

The following years, 1984 and 1985, might be expected to see sales in both markets reach 3 and 6 per cent respectively over their levels in 1979. The recovery from recession is likely to be relatively synchronised as between developed countries, so that there are grounds for expecting the main car markets to grow in parallel. This would yield total US sales in 1984 of 10.6 million units and in 1985, 10.9 million units. As for Western Europe, sales in 1983 of 10.7 million units would be followed by 1984 sales of 11.02 million units and sales in 1985 of 11.34 million units.

In Japan, where the pattern of the recession was very different after 1980 — in part due to the country's insulation from very high interest-rates — a rather different evolution is expected, with 1981 expected to have marked the trough of the recession as far as private consumption expenditure is concerned, and 1982 and 1983 building up to a new peak. In 1981 GNP overall rose by 2.9 per cent in Japan; in 1982 and 1983 growth of 2.0 and 4.0 per cent respectively is expected. However, real consumers' expenditure is likely to grow by substantially more than this, with 6 per cent growth in 1982 followed by nearly 8 per cent growth in 1983[1]. This could underwrite fairly substantial growth of car sales, so that the fairly quiet years of 1980 and 1981 (in which domestic registrations averaged 2,850,000 units) should give way to around 3 million sales in 1982 and 3.3 million in 1983. Indeed, 3.5 million units for both 1983 and 1984 are not unattainable targets. 1985 may see some slight downturn as economic growth comes off the boil a little, but even so 3.0 million units should be seen as a floor sales level for that year.

Given that imports account for a trivial 1.5 to 2 per cent of sales (and are not, despite recent public announcements, likely to grow much) the lion's share of the benefit of this growth will go straight to the Japanese producers.

The result of the upswing from the unexpectedly prolonged 1980-82 recession will not only be a rise in new car sales in most of the major markets, but will also be a much-needed recovery for the major firms' finances. During these last three years interest-rate charges on companies' debts have been very considerable, and these, coupled with the investment outlays from retained earnings needed to prepare for new models, have made many companies' operating environment very difficult. An upturn of sales on the scale envisaged here would go a long way to relieving firms'

---

1. OECD, *Economic Outlook,* July 1982 issue (Paris: OECD, 1982) p.83.

cash flow problems and allowing them to reorder their balance sheets.

What an upturn in new car sales in the major markets will not change, however, are the fundamentals of the industry as it approaches the end of the twentieth century. There is no question that the Japanese firms' competitiveness will continue to overhang every investment project undertaken in Europe and the US. Indeed, in the middle of 1982 there was ominous talk of Japanese firms being ready to start a round of price-cutting, to restore their slightly sagging market share in some countries. There are few in the industry who doubt their ability to do this if they so choose. A final factor to be borne in mind is that this competition from Japan is not restricted to the main markets: it extends to the growing third world markets too. And in many of them, particularly in Asia, the Japanese are extremely well-established, with large dealer networks and a reputation for reliability already won. The longer-established firms will have to work very hard indeed to keep up with the Japanese challenge.

CHART 9

CAR MARKET SALES FORECASTS TO 1985

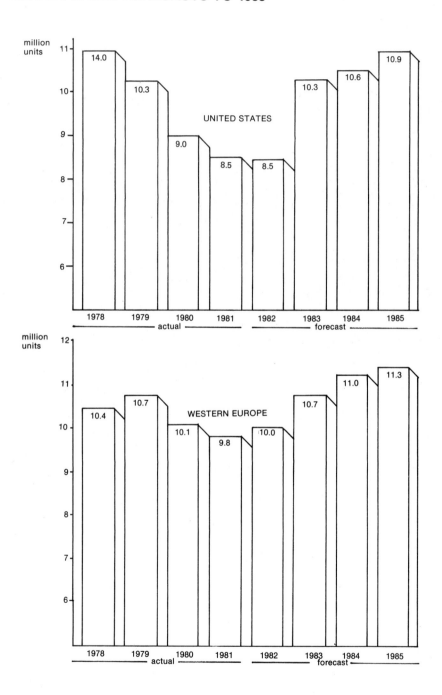

million
units

UNITED STATES

14.0 · 10.3 · 9.0 · 8.5 · 8.5 · 10.3 · 10.6 · 10.9

1978 1979 1980 1981 1982 1983 1984 1985
actual — forecast

million
units

WESTERN EUROPE

10.4 · 10.7 · 10.1 · 9.8 · 10.0 · 10.7 · 11.0 · 11.3

1978 1979 1980 1981 1982 1983 1984 1985
actual — forecast

CHART 10

IMPORTS SALES IN US AUTO MARKET (excluding imports from Canada)

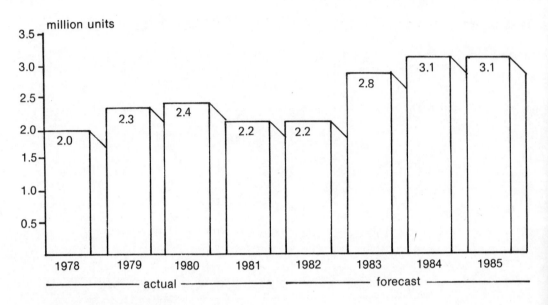

NEW REGISTRATIONS IN JAPAN

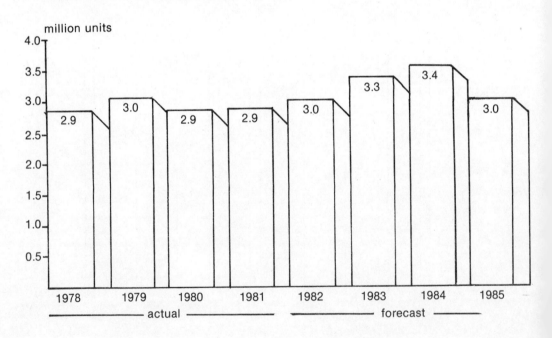

APPENDIX A

STATISTISTICAL SUPPLEMENT

Researched and Compiled by EUROMONITOR

1. Passenger Car Production in 1980 and 1981

2. Circulation of Passenger Cars 1977-1981

3. International Trade in Passenger Cars

4. New Car Registrations 1977-1981

General Note on Sources

Composite tables of figures for various countries have been drawn from statistics published by national statistical associations and motor trade organisations within the countries concerned, or from automotive trade journals.

1. PASSENGER CAR PRODUCTION IN 1980 AND 1981

SOURCES: l'Argus
World Automotive Market
United Nations
Statistical Offices: various countries
Motor trade associations
Euromonitor Estimates

TABLE 1

THE TOP TWENTY PASSENGER CAR MANUFACTURERS IN 1981

		'000s	% of world output
1	General Motors (USA)	3,904	14.3
2	Toyota (Japan)	2,248	8.2
3	Nissan (Japan)	1,864	6.8
4	Ford (USA)	1,320	4.8
5	Renault (France)	1,294	4.7
6	Volkswagen (West Germany)	1,151	4.2
7	Fiat (Italy)	878	3.2
8	Honda (Japan)	852	3.1
9	Mazda (Japan)	841	3.1
10	Lada (USSR)	830	3.0
11	Opel (France)	810	3.0
12	Chrysler (USA)	749	2.7
13	Mitsubishi (Japan)	607	2.2
14	Peugeot (France)	569	2.1
15	Citroen (France)	534	2.0
16	Ford (West Germany)	487	1.8
17	General Motors (Canada)	478	1.7
18	Daimler-Benz (West Germany)	449	1.6
19	BL (United Kingdom)	413	1.5
20	Ford (United Kingdom)	342	1.3

TABLE 2

THE TWENTY MAJOR CAR PRODUCING COUNTRIES IN 1981
('000 passenger cars)

		'000s	% of world output
1	Japan	6,974	25.5
2	USA	6,253	22.9
3	West Germany	3,578	13.1
4	France	2,612	9.6
5	USSR	1,350	4.9
6	Italy	1,257	4.6
7	United Kingdom	955	3.5
8	Spain	855	3.1
9	Canada	802	2.9
10	Brazil	593	2.2
11	Mexico	355	1.3
12	Poland	295	1.1
13	Yugoslavia	268	1.0
14	Sweden	250	0.9
15	Australia	214	0.8
16	Czechoslovakia	178	0.7
17	East Germany	177	0.6
18	Argentina	139	0.5
19	Netherlands	78	0.3
20	Romania	70	0.3

TABLE 3

REGIONAL SUMMARY : PASSENGER CAR PRODUCTION
('000s)

	1980	1981
a) Production		
Western Europe	10,196	9,617
Eastern Europe	2,427	2,354
North and Central America	7,526	7,410
South America	1,117	732
North Africa and Middle East	—	—
Africa	—	—
Far East	7,069	7,016
Oceania	182	214
TOTAL WORLD	28,517	27,343
b) Assembly		
Western Europe	300	325
Eastern Europe	—	—
North and Central America	10	10
South America	187	167
North Africa and Middle East	50	54
Africa	268	302
Far East	140	160
Oceania	73	96
TOTAL WORLD	1,028	1,114

TABLE 4

WESTERN EUROPE : SUMMARY OF PASSENGER CAR PRODUCTION BY COUNTRY
(units)

	1980	1981
a) Production		
France	2,938,581	2,611,864
Italy	1,445,221	1,257,340
Netherlands	80,779	77,922
Spain	1,028,813	855,325
Sweden	232,646	250,200
Turkey	25,486	31,529
United Kingdom	923,744	954,650
West Germany	3,520,934	3,577,807
b) Assembly		
Austria	7,000	7,500
Belgium	178,700	205,000
Eire	45,000	38,000
Finland	20,000	20,000
Greece	1,000	1,000
Portugal	45,457	60,910

TABLE 5

FRANCE

PASSENGER CAR PRODUCTION BY MAKE
(units)

	1980	1981
Renault	1,491,202	1,294,452
Peugeot	607,033	569,287
Citroen	536,366	533,922
Talbot	294,871	199,941
Talbot Matra	7,972	13,001
Alpine	1,137	1,261
TOTAL	2,938,581	2,611,864

Source : l'Argus

TABLE 6

ITALY

PASSENGER CAR PRODUCTION BY MAKE
(units)

	1980	1981
Fiat	995,455	878,365
Alfa Romeo	219,571	197,287
Lancia	110,756	78,257
Autobianchi	76,585	76,987
Innocenti	39,770	23,187
Maserati	555	528
Ferrari	2,381	2,566
De Tomaso	84	74
Lamborghini	64	89
TOTAL	1,445,221	1,257,340

Source : Anfia

TABLE 7

NETHERLANDS

PASSENGER CAR PRODUCTION BY MAKE
(units)

	1980	1981
Volvo	80,779	77,922
TOTAL	80,779	77,922

Source : RAI

TABLE 8

SPAIN

PASSENGER CAR PRODUCTION BY MAKE
(units)

	1980	1981
Fasa-Renault	324,680	269,029
Ford Espana	260,005	248,045
Seat	293,536	204,847
Citroen-Hispania	84,836	74,495
Talbot	65,756	58,909
TOTAL	1,028,813	855,325

Source : l'Argus

TABLE 9

SWEDEN

PASSENGER CAR PRODUCTION BY MAKE
(units)

	1980	1981
Saab	63,080	57,115
Volvo	169,566	193,085
TOTAL	232,646	250,200

Source : AB Bilstatisik

TABLE 10

TURKEY

PASSENGER CAR PRODUCTION BY MAKE
(units)

	1980	1981
Oyak — Renault	12,700	17,600
Tofas — Fiat	12,427	13,300
Otosan — Ford	359	629
TOTAL	25,486	31,529

Source : Otosan Otomobil Sanayii A S

TABLE 11

UNITED KINGDOM

PASSENGER CAR PRODUCTION BY MAKE
(units)

	1980	1981
British Leyland	395,820	413,440
Ford	342,767	342,171
Talbot	125,314	117,439
Vauxhall	55,002	69,932
De Lorean	—	7,409
Rolls Royce	3,108	3,087
Lotus	384	345
TVR	144	164
Reliant	582	89
Other	623	574
TOTAL	923,744	954,650

Source : SMMT

TABLE 12

WEST GERMANY

PASSENGER CAR PRODUCTION BY MAKE
(units)

	1980	1981
Volkswagen	1,232,164	1,150,560
Opel	786,663	810,158
Ford	419,517	486,917
Daimler-Benz	438,829	449,010
BMW	330,087	337,757
Audi	285,052	311,671
Porsche	28,622	31,734
TOTAL	3,520,934	3,577,807

Source : VDA

TABLE 13

EASTERN EUROPE : SUMMARY OF PASSENGER CAR PRODUCTION
(units)

	1980	1981
Production		
Bulgaria	15,000	16,000
Czechoslovakia	180,000	178,000
Romania	77,000	70,000
East Germany	175,000	176,500
Poland	355,000	295,000
USSR	1,330,000	1,350,000
Yugoslavia	294,887	268,413

TABLE 14

POLAND

PASSENGER CAR PRODUCTION BY MAKE
(units)

	1980	1981
Polski-Fiat	330,000	286,000
Syrena	25,000	9,000
TOTAL	355,000	295,000

Source : l'Argus

TABLE 15

USSR

PASSENGER CAR PRODUCTION BY MAKE
(units)

	1980	1981
Lada	825,000	830,000
Moskvitch	230,000	235,000
Volga	125,000	130,000
Saporoshje	150,000	155,000
TOTAL	1,330,000	1,350,000

Source : l'Argus

TABLE 16

YUGOSLAVIA

PASSENGER CAR PRODUCTION BY MAKE
(units)

	1980	1981
ZVZ	255,228	239,554
IMV	39,659	28,859
TOTAL	294,887	268,413

Source : BPMV

TABLE 17

NORTH AND CENTRAL AMERICA : SUMMARY OF PASSENGER CAR
PRODUCTION
(units)

	1980	1981
Production		
Canada	846,677	801,903
USA	6,375,506	6,253,138
Mexico	303,056	354,897
Assembly		
Trinidad and Tobago	10,150	10,000

TABLE 18

CANADA

PASSENGER CAR PRODUCTION BY MAKE
(units)

	1980	1981
General Motors	512,230	478,389
Ford	249,876	209,494
Chrysler	71,530	69,149
American Motors	3,077	34,535
Volvo	9,964	10,336
TOTAL	846,677	801,903

Source : MVMA (Canada)

TABLE 19

USA

PASSENGER CAR PRODUCTION BY MAKE
(units)

	1980	1981
General Motors	4,064,556	3,904,083
Ford	1,306,948	1,320,197
Chrysler	638,974	748,774
American Motors	164,725	109,319
Volkswagen	197,106	167,755
Checker	3,197	3,010
TOTAL	6,375,506	6,253,138

Source : MVMA (USA)

TABLE 20

MEXICO

PASSENGER CAR PRODUCTION BY MAKE
(units)

	1980	1981
Chrysler de Mexico	56,838	58,110
Ford	37,755	53,994
Nissan Mexicana	35,648	47,449
Volkswagen de Mexico	113,033	121,879
Other	59,782	73,465
TOTAL	303,056	354,897

Source : Associacon Mexicana de la Industria Automotriz

TABLE 21

SOUTH AMERICA : SUMMARY OF PASSENGER CAR PRODUCTION
(units)

	1980	1981
Production		
Argentina	218,513	139,428
Brazil	898,329	593,072
Assembly		
Chile	27,528	23,453
Colombia	32,280	24,732
Peru	10,700	13,096
Venezuela	115,965	105,881

TABLE 22

ARGENTINA

PASSENGER CAR PRODUCTION BY MAKE
(units)

	1980	1981
Ford	71,555	52,698
Renault	58,126	44,337
Fiat	34,446	12,868
Chrysler	27,771	17,326
Peugeot	26,615	12,199
TOTAL	218,513	139,428

Source : l'Argus

TABLE 23

BRAZIL

PASSENGER CAR PRODUCTION BY MAKE
(units)

	1980	1981
Volkswagen	425,000	265,000
General Motors	180,000	120,000
Fiat	162,000	125,000
Ford	120,000	80,000
Other	11,329	3,072
TOTAL	898,329	593,072

Source : Anfavea

TABLE 24

NORTH AFRICA AND MIDDLE EAST :
SUMMARY OF PASSENGER CAR PRODUCTION
(units)

	1980	1981
Production		
None		
Assembly		
Algeria	6,500	6,000
Egypt	16,000	19,500
Iran	50,000	50,000
Israel	1,650	1,750
Morocco	15,150	15,000
Tunisia	10,000	10,000

TABLE 25

**AFRICA : SUMMARY OF PASSENGER CAR PRODUCTION
(units)**

	1980	1981
Production		
None		
Assembly		
Ghana	1,000	1,000
Ivory Coast	7,500	8,000
Madagascar	1,500	1,200
Nigeria	55,000	50,000
Zaire	1,600	1,800
South Africa	268,300	301,528

TABLE 26

FAR EAST : SUMMARY OF PASSENGER CAR PRODUCTION
(units)

	1980	1981
Production		
India	30,538	42,106
Japan	7,038,108	6,974,131
Assembly		
Burma	1,000	1,000
China	70,000	75,000
Indonesia	20,000	18,000
Korea	57,225	68,760
Malaysia	81,355	87,823
Philippines	40,000	45,000
Thailand	12,000	15,000

TABLE 27

INDIA

PASSENGER CAR PRODUCTION BY MAKE
(units)

	1980	1981
Hindustan Motors	21,752	23,197
Premier Automobiles	8,729	18,874
Other	57	35
TOTAL	30,538	42,106

Source : All-India Automobile Industries Association

TABLE 28

JAPAN

PASSENGER CAR PRODUCTION BY MAKE
(units)

	1980	1981
Nissan	1,940,615	1,864,251
Toyota	2,303,284	2,248,171
Honda	845,514	852,177
Mazda	736,544	840,630
Mitsubishi	659,622	606,883
Suburu	202,038	190,451
Daihatsu	155,604	147,219
Isuzu	107,057	129,564
Suzuki	87,830	94,785
TOTAL	7,038,108	6,974,131

Source : Japan Automobile Manufacturers Association

TABLE 29

OCEANIA : SUMMARY OF PASSENGER CAR PRODUCTION
(units)

	1980	1981
Production		
Australia	182,000	213,500
Assembly		
New Zealand	73,400	95,500

TABLE 30

AUSTRALIA

PASSENGER CAR PRODUCTION BY MAKE
(units)

	1980	1981
Ford	80,000	110,000
Holden-Bedford	98,000	99,000
Chrysler	4,000	4,500
TOTAL	182,000	213,500

Source : ABS

2. CIRCULATION OF PASSENGER CARS 1977-1981

SOURCES : l'Argus
World Automotive Market
Motor Vehicle Manufacturers Association (USA)
Society of Motor Manufacturers & Traders (GB)
Other motor trade associations
United Nations
Euromonitor Estimates

TABLE 31

REGIONAL SUMMARY : PASSENGER CARS IN CIRCULATION

(million cars)	1978	1979	1980	1981	1982
Western Europe	94.3	97.2	101.8	105.4	108.7
Eastern Europe	15.1	17.2	18.7	20.4	21.4
North & Central America	127.9	131.6	135.4	138.9	140.4
South America	11.6	12.4	13.2	14.3	14.9
North Africa & Middle East	3.4	4.2	4.7	5.3	5.7
Africa	4.2	4.5	4.8	4.9	5.2
Far East	23.4	25.3	27.0	28.5	29.5
Oceania	6.9	7.0	7.2	7.3	7.5
TOTAL	286.8	299.4	312.8	325.0	333.3

(persons per car)	1978	1979	1980	1981	1982
Western Europe	4.2	4.1	3.9	3.8	3.7
Eastern Europe	26.1	23.1	21.2	19.9	19.0
North & Central America	2.7	2.7	2.7	2.7	2.7
South America	20.1	19.3	18.7	17.8	17.1
North Africa & Middle East	38.2	31.9	29.3	26.4	24.5
Africa	88.1	84.7	81.7	81.6	76.8
Far East	95.6	90.0	85.8	82.5	79.7
Oceania	3.3	3.3	3.2	3.2	3.1
TOTAL WORLD	14.4	14.1	13.7	13.6	13.3

Note: At January 1st of each year

TABLE 32

CIRCULATION
('000s at January 1st)

REGION ONE : WESTERN EUROPE

	1978	1979	1980	1981	1982
Austria	1,965	2,040	2,139	2,247	2,309
Belgium	2,871	2,973	3,077	3,151	3,210
Cyprus	72	79	86	92	100
Denmark	1,375	1,408	1,423	1,390	1,367
Finland	1,069	1,108	1,170	1,218	1,271
France	16,990	17,720	18,440	19,130	19,750
Germany, West	20,377	21,620	22,614	23,236	23,681
Greece	742	790	839	880	920
Iceland	67	73	76	81	84
Ireland	574	640	683	734	775
Italy	16,466	16,241	17,023	17,696	18,450
Luxembourg	141	153	164	173	180
Malta	56	64	67	66	68
Netherlands	3,950	3,851	4,200	4,300	4,600
Norway	1,107	1,147	1,190	1,234	1,279
Portugal	862	888	912	941	990
Spain	5,945	6,530	7,058	7,557	7,943
Sweden	2,857	2,856	2,868	2,883	2,893
Switzerland	1,933	2,055	2,154	2,247	2,515
Turkey	532	596	658	702	715
United Kingdom	14,355	14,417	14,927	15,438	15,632
TOTAL	94,306	97,249	101,768	105,396	108,732

TABLE 33

CIRCULATION
('000s at January 1st)

REGION TWO : EASTERN EUROPE

	1978	1979	1980	1981	1982
Bulgaria	220	350	480	500	520
Czechoslovakia	1,836	1,900	1,977	1,950	2,000
Hungary	738	851	913	1,012	1,096
Germany, East	2,237	2,392	2,480	2,678	2,800
Poland	1,290	1,835	2,117	2,383	2,500
Romania	220	230	235	250	260
USSR	6,644	7,494	8,255	9,250	9,700
Yugoslavia	1,924	2,134	2,285	2,417	2,563
TOTAL	15,109	17,186	18,742	20,440	21,439

TABLE 34

CIRCULATION
('000s at January 1st)

REGION THREE : NORTH AND CENTRAL AMERICA

	1978	1979	1980	1981	1982
Bahamas	38	42	44	46	48
Barbados	24	25	24	25	26
Canada	9,841	10,080	10,226	10,367	10,710
Costa Rica	60	62	80	90	95
Cuba	80	80	80	80	80
Guadeloupe	46	49	52	53	55
Guatemala	101	124	131	160	180
Haiti	21	23	25	32	35
Honduras	20	36	25	27	30
Jamaica	107	105	106	108	110
Mexico	2,580	2,829	3,010	3,323	3,500
Nicaragua	35	38	40	38	40
Panama	87	89	92	93	95
Puerto Rico	649	699	850	870	900
Trinidad & Tobago	112	122	135	140	146
USA	114,113	117,147	120,485	123,467	124,336
TOTAL	127,914	131,550	135,405	138,919	140,386

124

TABLE 35

CIRCULATION
('000s at January 1st)

REGION FOUR : SOUTH AMERICA

	1978	1979	1980	1981	1982
Argentina	2,588	2,649	2,730	2,950	3,176
Bolivia	32	33	35	32	35
Brazil	6,349	6,927	7,504	8,149	8,400
Chile	289	328	376	405	415
Colombia	452	490	509	552	575
Dominican Republic	83	88	90	90	92
Ecuador	61	66	70	65	70
Guyana	31	32	33	33	35
Paraguay	29	28	32	34	35
Peru	312	312	312	319	330
Uruguay	166	163	168	173	182
Venezuela	1,172	1,269	1,390	1,464	1,550
TOTAL	11,564	12,385	13,249	14,266	14,895

TABLE 36

CIRCULATION
('000s at January 1st)

REGION FIVE : NORTH AFRICA AND MIDDLE EAST

	1978	1979	1980	1981	1982
Algeria	339	317	397	490	525
Iran	728	1,020	1,028	1,079	1,150
Iraq	98	99	121	163	180
Israel	313	334	350	403	415
Jordan	61	73	79	90	97
Kuwait	274	321	363	399	450
Lebanon	230	282	315	362	350
Libya	300	315	360	367	372
Morocco	264	372	380	425	450
Oman	23	22	30	40	45
Qatar	31	45	36	44	50
Saudi Arabia	376	478	613	764	850
Syria	57	62	74	65	70
UAR	204	324	379	445	500
Tunisia	105	107	111	112	115
Yemen	14	15	15	16	18
Yemen, South	12	12	12	13	14
TOTAL	3,429	4,198	4,663	5,277	5,651

TABLE 37

CIRCULATION
('000s at January 1st)

REGION SIX : AFRICA

	1978	1979	1980	1981	1982
Angola	147	143	144	142	145
Benin	14	16	22	22	25
Botswana	5	5	6	8	9
Burundi	5	6	6	6	7
Cameroon	52	55	63	67	70
Central AR	14	15	15	15	16
Chad	8	8	8	8	9
Congo	21	20	20	20	22
Egypt	270	324	379	428	450
Ethiopia	44	43	38	40	42
Gambia	5	7	9	10	13
Ghana	56	62	67	66	68
Ivory Coast	92	112	115	128	135
Kenya	93	118	122	127	129
Liberia	20	22	22	22	24
Madagascar	55	55	57	56	58
Malawi	15	16	16	16	17
Mali	21	22	22	22	23
Mauritius	31	32	32	32	33
Mozambique	53	105	102	99	105
Niger	13	13	13	16	18
Nigeria	361	404	443	522	600
Senegal	50	56	58	59	60
South Africa	2,244	2,343	2,331	2,456	2,600
Sudan	28	30	35	35	36
Tanzania	34	43	42	43	45
Togo	17	19	19	20	21
Uganda	32	32	32	33	35
Upper Volta	12	12	12	13	15
Zaire	84	95	94	94	95
Zambia	90	105	104	103	105
Zimbabwe	165	172	175	172	180
TOTAL	4,151	4,510	4,795	4,900	5,210

TABLE 38

CIRCULATION
('000s at January 1st)

REGION SEVEN : FAR EAST

	1978	1979	1980	1981	1982
Afghanistan	36	35	37	34	33
Bangladesh	26	27	27	27	28
Burma	33	32	33	38	40
China	47	50	60	60	65
Hong Kong	132	153	173	205	223
India	711	802	919	949	990
Indonesia	443	540	577	630	722
Japan	19,826	21,280	22,667	23,660	24,612
Korea, South	126	185	241	249	267
Laos	15	15	15	15	16
Malaysia	503	567	596	629	650
Pakistan	192	209	264	286	300
Philippines	431	453	469	479	495
Singapore	136	146	143	165	175
Sri Lanka	97	104	114	121	127
Taiwan	295	314	318	338	350
Thailand	344	370	387	397	420
TOTAL	23,393	25,282	27,040	28,282	29,513

TABLE 39

CIRCULATION
('000s at January 1st)

REGION EIGHT : OCEANIA

	1978	1979	1980	1981	1982
Australia	5,604	5,642	5,815	5,950	6,080
Fiji	25	26	26	27	28
New Caledonia	31	32	36	38	40
New Zealand	1,230	1,247	1,277	1,297	1,339
Papua New Guinea	20	21	22	24	25
TOTAL	6,910	6,968	7,176	7,336	7,512

TABLE 40

PERSONS PER PASSENGER CAR : WESTERN EUROPE

U.S. = 1.8 ↓

	1978	1979	1980	1981	1982
Austria	3.8	3.7	3.5	3.3	3.3
Belgium	3.4	3.3	3.2	3.1	3.1
Cyprus	8.6	7.9	7.3	6.8	6.3
Denmark	3.7	3.6	3.6	3.7	3.7
Finland	4.4	4.3	4.1	3.9	3.8
France	5.0	3.0	2.9	2.8	2.7 ✓④
Germany, West	3.1	2.8	2.7	2.6	2.6 ✓③
Greece	12.6	12.0	11.4	10.9	10.4
Iceland	3.3	3.0	3.0	2.8	2.7
Ireland	5.8	5.3	5.0	4.6	4.4
Italy	3.4	3.5	3.3	3.2	3.1
Luxembourg	2.6	2.3	2.2	2.1	2.0 ✓①
Malta	6.1	5.5	5.4	5.4	5.3
Netherlands	3.5	3.6	3.4	3.3	3.1
Norway	3.7	3.5	3.4	3.3	3.2
Portugal	11.6	11.1	10.9	10.5	10.0
Spain	6.2	15.0	5.3	4.9	4.7
Sweden	2.9	2.9	2.9	2.9	2.9
Switzerland	3.3	3.1	3.0	2.8	2.5 ✓ⓔ
Turkey	81.1	74.2	68.3	64.1	63.3
United Kingdom	3.9	3.9	3.7	3.6	3.6

TABLE 41

PERSONS PER PASSENGER CAR : EASTERN EUROPE

	1978	1979	1980	1981	1982
Bulgaria	40.0	25.6	18.4	17.7	17.0
Czechoslovakia	8.2	8.0	6.7	7.9	7.7
Hungary	14.5	12.6	11.7	10.6	9.8
Germany, East	7.5	5.8	4.8	6.3	6.0
Poland	27.1	19.2	16.7	14.9	14.2
Romania	99.3	95.9	94.8	89.0	85.7
USSR	39.3	35.1	32.1	28.7	27.4
Yugoslavia	11.4	10.3	9.8	9.2	8.7

TABLE 42

PERSONS PER PASSENGER CAR : NORTH AND CENTRAL AMERICA

	1978	1979	1980	1981	1982
Bahamas	6.0	5.3	5.4	4.9	5.0
Barbados	11.2	10.0	10.4	10.0	9.6
Canada	2.4	2.3	2.3	2.3	2.2
Costa Rica	35.3	35.0	28.0	24.9	23.6
Cuba	121.1	122.1	122.9	122.9	12.9
Guadeloupe	6.7	6.5	6.3	6.2	6.0
Guatemala	67.7	56.8	55.4	45.4	40.3
Haiti	230.0	213.9	200.4	156.6	143.1
Honduras	172.0	95.6	147.6	136.7	123.0
Jamaica	19.8	20.6	20.7	20.3	20.0
Mexico	25.9	24.5	23.9	21.6	20.6
Nicaragua	68.9	69.5	67.5	71.1	67.5
Panama	20.1	20.1	20.0	19.8	19.4
Puerto Rico	5.2	4.9	4.0	3.9	3.9
Trinidad & Tobago	10.1	9.3	8.4	8.1	7.9
USA	1.9	1.9	1.9	1.8	1.8

TABLE 43

PERSONS PER PASSENGER CAR : SOUTH AMERICA

	1978	1979	1980	1981	1982
Argentina	10.2	10.1	9.9	9.2	8.5
Bolivia	165.3	155.1	160.0	175.0	160.0
Brazil	18.2	17.1	16.4	15.1	14.6
Chile	37.1	33.3	29.5	27.4	26.7
Columbia	56.7	53.8	53.2	49.1	47.1
Dominican Republic	61.7	60.0	60.3	60.3	59.0
Ecuador	129.5	122.4	119.3	128.5	121.4
Guyana	26.5	27.2	26.7	26.7	25.4
Paraguay	99.7	106.1	95.9	90.3	87.7
Peru	52.6	54.0	57.0	55.7	53.9
Uruguay	17.2	17.7	17.3	16.8	15.9
Venezuela	11.2	10.7	10.0	9.5	9.0

TABLE 44

PERSONS PER PASSENGER CAR : NORTH AFRICA AND MIDDLE EAST

	1978	1979	1980	1981	1982
Algeria	51.4	57.4	46.8	37.9	35.7
Iran	48.8	36.2	36.4	34.7	32.6
Iraq	125.8	129.0	108.1	80.7	72.7
Israel	11.8	11.3	11.1	9.6	9.4
Jordan	48.8	44.3	40.4	35.4	32.9
Kuwait	4.4	4.0	3.7	3.4	3.1
Lebanon	13.0	11.0	10.0	8.6	9.1
Libya	9.1	9.1	8.3	8.1	8.2
Morocco	71.6	52.3	53.3	47.6	45.1
Oman	36.5	39.1	29.7	22.2	20.0
Qatar	6.4	4.7	6.1	5.0	4.6
Saudi Arabia	20.9	17.0	13.6	11.0	10.0
Syria	146.1	139.5	140.3	138.1	130.0
UAR	3.5	2.3	2.1	1.8	1.6
Tunisia	57.9	58.3	57.4	56.9	55.6
Yemen	403.6	386.0	395.3	370.6	330.0
Yemen, South	154.2	157.5	161.7	149.2	141.4

TABLE 45

PERSONS PER PASSENGER CAR : AFRICA

	1978	1979	1980	1981	1982
Angola	45.8	68.0	49.2	49.9	49.3
Benin	241.4	216.9	162.3	162.3	144.0
Botswana	152.0	131.7	136.7	102.5	91.0
Burundi	81.9	76.6	75.6	67.3	68.4
Cameroon	155.0	150.0	134.9	126.9	122.0
Central AR	151.4	144.7	148.0	145.5	140.6
Chad	538.7	552.5	565.0	568.0	502.0
Congo	69.5	75.0	77.0	77.0	71.8
Egypt	147.5	126.5	110.8	98.1	93.3
Ethiopia	675.2	707.4	817.6	776.8	739.8
Gambia	114.0	82.86	66.65	61.0	48.1
Ghana	195.9	182.6	170.9	173.5	169.1
Ivory Coast	82.7	70.7	65.3	62.8	59.3
Kenya	159.8	129.8	134.4	129.1	127.0
Liberia	86.0	80.4	85.0	85.0	80.0
Madagascar	150.7	154.7	153.3	156.1	150.0
Malawi	378.0	264.5	373.1	373.1	352.5
Mali	312.4	305.9	314.1	314.1	304.5
Mauritius	29.0	28.4	30.0	30.0	30.0
Mozambique	187.5	97.1	102.6	105.8	101.0
Niger	383.8	396.1	408.5	331.8	297.0
Nigeria	200.0	184.6	174.0	147.7	133.3
Senegal	107.6	98.4	97.6	95.9	95.0
South Africa	12.3	12.2	12.6	11.9	11.5
Sudan	620.7	596.3	534.0	534.0	519.0
Tanzania	512.9	418.1	438.1	427.9	414.0
Togo	141.8	130.0	142.1	135.0	135.0
Uganda	399.4	413.1	412.5	400.0	378.6
Upper Volta	545.8	560.8	575.8	531.5	466.5
Zaire	322.4	293.4	301.0	301.0	300.0
Zambia	60.8	53.8	56.1	56.6	56.2
Zimbabwe	40.6	39.5	39.0	41.0	39.0

TABLE 46

PERSONS PER PASSENGER CAR : FAR EAST

	1978	1979	1980	1981	1982
Afghanistan	353.3	372.9	360.8	392.6	405.0
Bangladesh	3,256.1	3,208.9	3,246.7	3,246.7	3,132.4
Burma	976.1	1,028.4	1,069.7	928.9	900.0
China	19,851.7	18,900.4	15,947.5	15,947.5	14,800.0
Hong Kong	34.9	32.0	29.3	24.7	23.0
India	897.9	811.7	722.1	699.3	675.0
Indonesia	317.5	274.9	263.2	240.1	205.0
Japan	5.8	5.5	5.2	4.9	4.8
Korea, South	293.8	203.2	158.5	153.4	146.0
Laos	236.7	242.0	248.0	248.0	235.0
Malaysia	25.7	23.5	22.5	21.2	20.8
Pakistan	399.8	382.0	312.3	288.2	276.7
Philippines	105.6	102.8	103.2	101.0	100.0
Singapore	17.1	16.2	16.7	14.5	13.7
Sri Lanka	146.3	139.1	129.3	121.8	117.0
Taiwan	58.1	55.7	55.4	52.1	50.3
Thailand	131.1	124.7	121.9	118.8	114.9

TABLE 47

PERSONS PER PASSENGER CAR : OCEANIA

	1978	1979	1980	1981	1982
Australia	2.5	2.6	2.5	2.5	2.4
Fiji	24.4	23.6	24.2	23.3	22.9
New Caledonia	4.8	4.4	5.8	5.6	3.7
New Zealand	2.5	2.5	2.4	2.4	2.4
Papua New Guinea	149.5	146.7	140.0	128.3	123.6

3. INTERNATIONAL TRADE IN PASSENGER CARS

SOURCES : External Trade manuals — various countries
Motor trade associations
O.E.C.D.
United Nations

TABLE 48

EUROPE : IMPORTS OF PASSENGER CARS IN VALUE
(unit: $ million)

	1977	1978	1979	1980	1981
Western Europe					
Austria	1,200	746	1,140	1,276	903
Belgium/Luxembourg	1,349	1,734	2,209	2,247	
Cyprus	27	32	38	43	
Denmark	397	481	513	260	
Finland	191	202	291	339	
France	1,732	2,112	2,636	3,244	3,345
Germany, West	3,391	4,604	5,066	4,832	3,875
Greece	188	344	426	314	
Iceland	23	29	28	28	
Ireland	232	399	456	470	
Italy	1,421	1,966	2,832	4,597	3,949
Malta	8	13	15	21	
Netherlands	1,936	2,402	2,803	1,738	
Norway	514	257	426	415	
Portugal	16	45	127	190	
Spain	64	71	172	362	
Sweden	698	591	801	748	
Switzerland	987	1,539	1,716	1,706	
United Kingdom	2,317	3,404	5,525	4,895	
Eastern Europe					
Poland	59	83	88	50	
Yugoslavia	165	176	271	183	

TABLE 49

NORTH AND CENTRAL AMERICA :
IMPORTS OF PASSENGER CARS IN VALUE
(unit: $ million)

	1977	1978	1979	1980
Bahamas	1	1	—	1
Barbados	5	4	4	4
Canada	3,203	3,279	3,832	3,827
Costa Rica	29	30	35	—
Guadeloupe	19	23	32	26
Guatemala	16	32	33	44
Haiti	4	6	6	7
Honduras	9	12	15	18
Jamaica	4	5	13	11
Nicaragua	26	13	3	9
Panama	15	23	40	—
Trinidad & Tobago	43	56	54	73
USA	11,182	14,866	16,016	18,017

TABLE 50

SOUTH AMERICA : IMPORTS OF PASSENGER CARS IN VALUE
(unit: $ million)

	1977	1978	1979	1980
Chile	67	68	117	203
Colombia	28	31	46	—
Dominican Republic	19	16	16	21
Ecuador	6	44	—	—
Guyana	2	1	2	1
Paraguay	11	13	14	12
Peru	57	—	—	—
Uruguay	21	22	58	—
Venezuela	427	580	551	—

TABLE 51

NORTH AFRICA AND MIDDLE EAST :
IMPORTS OF PASSENGER CARS IN VALUE
(unit: $ million)

	1977	1978	1979	1980
Algeria	74	117	27	
Iran	322	459	127	
Iraq	75	70	170	
Israel	75	119	178	
Jordan	44	58	70	
Kuwait	292	298	345	
Libya	175	247	308	
Morocco	66	52	63	
Oman	71	104	128	210
Qatar	91	86	92	129
Saudi Arabia	268	703	936	1,340
Syria	13	12	11	
UAR	141	138	164	
Tunisia	8	12	17	
Yemen	30	50	42	
Yemen, South	6	—	—	

TABLE 52

AFRICA : IMPORTS OF PASSENGER CARS IN VALUE
(unit: $ million)

	1977	1978	1979	1980
Burundi	3	4	4	5
Cameroon	23	30	34	35
Central African Rep	2	2	1	2
Congo	5	5	5	6
Ethiopia	9	9	11	12
Gambia	2	2	3	3
Ghana	31			
Ivory Coast	44	54	58	
Kenya	30	52		
Liberia	14	19	22	25
Madagascar	4	4	8	8
Malawi	3	7	8	10
Mali	5	5	6	6
Mauritius	13	13	12	14
Nigeria	461	353	325	
Senegal	19	26	24	17
South Africa	289	432	423	
Sudan	15	10		
Tanzania	4	8	10	
Togo	8	7	8	8
Upper Volta	4	6	7	8
Zaire	9	10	17	20
Zambia	2	5		3

TABLE 53

FAR EAST : IMPORTS OF PASSENGER CARS IN VALUE
(unit: $ million)

	1977	1978	1979	1980
Afghanistan	6	5	5	6
Bangladesh	7	13	11	12
Burma	1	1	1	2
Hong Kong	85	144	164	220
India	45	54		
Indonesia	69	101	98	167
Japan	285	398	310	452
Malaysia	231	270	227	
Pakistan	32	44	31	68
Philippines	69	96	102	
Singapore	94	146	165	209
Sri Lanka	6	19	28	18
Thailand	67	75	70	

TABLE 54

OCEANIA : IMPORTS OF PASSENGER CARS IN VALUE
(unit: $ million)

	1977	1978	1979	1980
Australia	518	544	577	529
Fiji	4	7	8	8
New Caledonia	16	21	21	29
New Zealand	154	159	256	243

TABLE 55

EUROPE : EXPORTS OF PASSENGER CARS IN VALUE
(unit: $ million)

	1977	1978	1979	1980	1981
Western Europe					
Austria	20	20	66	159	143
Belgium/Luxembourg	3,158	4,075	4,750	4,599	4,182
Cyprus	3	4	4	5	6
Denmark	30	28	42	75	
Finland	69	68	71	74	
France	4,563	5,549	7,165	6,748	5,523
Germany, West	9,598	11,831	14,180	14,582	13,697
Ireland	21	19	93	122	
Italy	1,961	2,301	2,771	2,448	1,619
Malta	1	2	2	2	
Netherlands	207	236	334	383	
Norway	1	1	5	1	2
Portugal					45
Spain	596	868	1,193	1,496	1,172
Sweden	660	945	1,286	1,197	1,071
Switzerland	9	9	9	19	
Turkey	1	1	3	4	
United Kingdom	1,352	1,814	1,779	1,944	
Eastern Europe					
Poland	84	152	139	197	
USSR	807	839	879		
Yugoslavia	36	44	61	128	

TABLE 56

THE AMERICAS : EXPORTS OF PASSENGER CARS IN VALUE
(unit: $ million)

	1977	1978	1979	1980	1981
Canada	4,034	4,124	3,669	3,966	4,715
Guadeloupe	2	1	1	1	
Mexico	58	64	60		
Panama	1	1	2	3	
USA	3,702	3,837	4,642	3,932	3,928
Argentina	56	35	25		
Brazil	82	183	17		
Colombia	11	15	4	6	
Uruguay	1	2	4	4	

TABLE 57

**AFRICA AND MIDDLE EAST : EXPORTS OF PASSENGER CARS IN VALUE
(unit: $ million)**

	1977	1978	1979	1980
Jordan	2	2	2	
Kuwait	59	64	21	
Lebanon	1	1	3	3
Oman	1	1	34	67
Qatar	5	5	7	8
Saudi Arabia	32	33	74	116
UAR	12	8	7	7
Yemen	—	1	1	1
South Africa	10	20	28	

TABLE 58

FAR EAST AND OCEANIA : EXPORTS OF PASSENGER CARS IN VALUE
(unit: $ million)

	1977	1978	1979	1980
Hong Kong	10	18	23	33
India	1	1	2	2
Japan	8,004	10,617	11,964	16,115
Korea, South	15	42	54	50
Singapore	47	69	61	89
Australia	42	41	81	81

TABLE 59

WESTERN EUROPE : IMPORTS OF PASSENGER CARS IN VOLUME
(unit: '000s)

	1977	1978	1979	1980	1981
Austria	313	158	222	232	192
Belgium/Luxembourg	346	345	399	361	354
Cyprus	9	9	10	10	9
Denmark	135	141	143	73	78
Finland	78	70	87	96	95
France	575	564	612	684	795
Germany, West	960	1,069	1,056	1,027	947
Greece	77	75	61	30	44
Iceland	3	4	4	5	7
Ireland	87	112	97	70	78
Italy	478	531	648	941	898
Malta	4	5	5	5	5
Netherlands	592	575	608	366	383
Norway	158	66	103	102	109
Portugal	1	3	11	6	9
Spain	13	12	27	51	54
Sweden	179	132	162	142	133
Switzerland	251	287	299	293	306
Turkey	3	26	1	1	1
United Kingdom	678	801	1,061	863	858

152

TABLE 60

**EASTERN EUROPE : IMPORTS OF PASSENGER CARS IN VOLUME
(unit: '000s)**

	1977	1978	1979	1980	1981
Bulgaria	82	83	87	81	
Czechoslovakia	76	86	78	58	21
Hungary	95	108	109	109	101
Germany, East	83	94	58	62	
Poland	32	44	41	22	
Romania	7	13	14	19	
Yugoslavia	60	65	72	47	45

TABLE 61

NORTH AND CENTRAL AFRICA :
IMPORTS OF PASSENGER CARS IN VOLUME
(unit: '000s)

	1977	1978	1979	1980	1981
Bahamas	3	5	3	3	3
Barbados	1	1	2	2	3
Canada	792	742	707	702	724
Costa Rica	3	4	6	8	2
Guadeloupe	5	4	4	3	4
Guatemala	8	9	7	5	3
Haiti	2	3	2	2	2
Honduras	3	3	2	2	2
Jamaica	2	2	6	3	4
Mexico	75	110	62	50	41
Nicaragua	5	2	1	1	—
Panama	3	4	7	11	9
Puerto Rico	42	45	43	75	59
Trinidad & Tobago	10	15	13	16	13
USA	2,892	3,025	3,006	3,248	2,999

TABLE 62

SOUTH AMERICA : IMPORTS OF PASSENGER CARS IN VOLUME
(unit: '000s)

	1977	1978	1979	1980	1981
Argentina	5	5	20	62	51
Bolivia	2	3	1	2	5
Brazil	30	50	83	130	175
Chile	34	19	35	62	94
Colombia	24	25	27	30	22
Dominican Republic	8	6	9	9	3
Ecuador	7	8	6	7	5
Guyana	1	1	1	1	1
Paraguay	2	4	5	14	3
Peru	6	3	6	12	25
Uruguay	1	2	4	12	10
Venezuela	83	91	59	58	20

TABLE 63

NORTH AFRICA AND MIDDLE EAST :
IMPORTS OF PASSENGER CARS IN VOLUME
(unit: '000s)

	1977	1978	1979	1980	1981
Algeria	5	2	4	22	21
Iran	170	167	41	83	19
Iraq	5	6	27	49	61
Israel	22	29	37	14	55
Jordan	23	16	17	19	21
Kuwait	53	42	49	45	38
Lebanon	5	5	7	11	7
Libya	46	62	65	20	61
Morocco	27	19	21	17	13
Oman	9	6	9	40	15
Qatar	6	5	6	9	9
Saudi Arabia	111	140	149	171	144
Syria	5	6	5	3	2
UAR	29	22	25	7	31
Tunisia	3	5	4	6	5
Yemen	2	2	2	1	1
Yemen, South	1	1	1	1	1

TABLE 64

AFRICA : IMPORTS OF PASSENGER CARS IN VOLUME
(unit: '000s)

	1977	1978	1979	1980	1981
Angola	1	2	3	3	1
Benin	1	1	1	1	2
Botswana	—	1	1	—	—
Burundi	1	1	1	1	1
Cameroon	—	7	6	7	6
Central African Rep	1	1	1	1	1
Chad	1	1	1	—	—
Congo	—	1	1	1	1
Egypt	19	25	28	19	16
Ethiopia	1	2	2	1	1
Gambia	—	1	1	—	—
Ghana	3	3	1	1	1
Ivory Coast	14	17	15	17	11
Kenya	7	11	7	10	4
Liberia	4	4	2	2	2
Madagascar	1	1	2	1	1
Malawi	1	1	1	1	1
Mali	1	1	1	1	1
Mauritius	5	1	1	1	1
Mozambique	—	1	1	—	1
Niger	—	1	1	2	1
Nigeria	82	79	54	93	130
Senegal	5	4	4	3	2
South Africa	119	158	103	102	85
Sudan	3	3	2	1	1
Tanzania	1	3	3	2	1
Togo	2	2	2	3	2
Uganda	1	1	1	2	1
Upper Volta	1	1	1	1	1
Zaire	2	3	4	3	3
Zambia	2	1	3	4	2

TABLE 65

FAR EAST : IMPORTS OF PASSENGER CARS IN VOLUME
(unit: '000s)

	1977	1978	1979	1980	1981
Afghanistan	2	2	1	—	—
Bangladesh	2	3	2	1	1
Burma	1	—	1	1	1
China	—	1	2	2	2
Hong Kong	23	34	37	49	38
India	1	1	2	3	3
Indonesia	17	19	15	27	31
Japan	41	55	65	46	32
Korea, South	18	29	6	1	2
Malaysia	75	88	83	104	111
Pakistan	17	30	12	19	12
Philippines	—	22	32	27	28
Singapore	33	40	45	59	38
Sri Lanka	3	4	3	3	3
Taiwan	36	62	34	33	17
Thailand	28	30	27	26	31

TABLE 66

OCEANIA : IMPORTS OF PASSENGER CARS IN VOLUME
(unit: '000s)

	1977	1978	1979	1980	1981
Australia	84	82	87	95	109
Fiji	1	2	2	2	3
New Caledonia	3	3	4	4	3
New Zealand	61	49	76	75	77
Papua New Guinea	2	3	3	4	3

TABLE 67

**WESTERN EUROPE : EXPORTS OF PASSENGER CARS IN VOLUME
(unit: '000s)**

	1977	1978	1979	1980	1981
Austria	1	1	3	7	6
Belgium	960	1,051	986	839	820
Cyprus	1	1	1	1	2
Denmark	—	—	—	17	—
Finland	15	13	14	11	12
France	1,621	1,579	1,697	1,530	1,394
Germany, West	1,939	1,904	1,997	1,874	1,950
Ireland	—	—	—	25	—
Italy	644	675	687	511	424
Malta	—	1	1	—	—
Netherlands	57	61	56	74	80
Portugal	—	—	—	3	—
Spain	333	406	434	526	462
Sweden	163	192	188	156	167
Switzerland	4	2	5	7	9
Turkey	—	—	—	5	—
United Kingdom	475	466	410	359	305

TABLE 68

EASTERN EUROPE : EXPORTS OF PASSENGER CARS IN VOLUME
(unit: '000s)

	1977	1978	1979	1980	1981
Czechoslovakia	74	87	82	81	97
Germany, East	77	92	89	85	
Poland	90	81	88	77	
Romania	19	17	19	14	12
USSR	362	403	395	343	
Yugoslavia	24	39	31		

TABLE 69

OTHER REGIONS : EXPORTS OF PASSENGER CARS IN VOLUME
(unit: '000s)

	1977	1978	1979	1980	1981
Canada	920	874	675	626	619
Mexico	5	22	15	13	13
USA	688	672	741	560	506
Argentina	4	1	2	3	3
Brazil	59	80	95	115	—
India	1	1	1	1	2
Japan	3,030	3,166	3,375	4,352	3,947
Korea, South	5	30	19	15	17
Singapore	16	21	19	28	—
Australia	18	30	3	4	3

4. NEW PASSENGER CAR REGISTRATIONS

SOURCES : Statistical Offices, various countries
Motor Trade Associations, various countries

TABLE 70

NEW REGISTRATIONS
(unit: '000s)

WESTERN EUROPE

	1977	1978	1979	1980	1981
Austria	296	158	214	227	199
Belgium	429	424	429	399	351
Cyprus	8	9	10	9	10
Denmark	141	133	127	74	72
Finland	90	81	100	103	108
France	1,907	1,945	1,976	1,873	1,835 ²
Germany, West	2,561	2,663	2,623	2,426	2,330 ˙
Greece	110	120	88	42	50
Iceland	6	8	8	8	8
Ireland	82	106	96	94	103
Italy	1,219	1,194	1,397	1,530	1,806 ³
Luxembourg	21	22	23	22	23
Malta	4	4	5	4	4
Netherlands	552	585	575	450	389
Norway	145	78	89	96	105
Portugal	76	53	52	58	61
Spain	663	654	621	542	475 ⁵
Sweden	241	201	215	193	189
Switzerland	234	272	280	222	303
Turkey	65	61	55	52	55
United Kingdom	1,324	1,592	1,716	1,514	1,485 ⁴

TABLE 71

NEW REGISTRATIONS
(unit: '000s)

EASTERN EUROPE

	1977	1978	1979	1980
Bulgaria	80	83	83	78
Czechoslovakia	134	162	146	112
Hungary	94	107	109	113
Germany, East	151	161	126	139
Poland	227	262	247	193
Romania	65	73	71	84
USSR	1,107	1,182	1,105	1,163

TABLE 72

NEW REGISTRATIONS
(unit: '000s)

NORTH AND CENTRAL AMERICA

	1977	1978	1979	1980	1981
Canada	991	988	1,003	932	904
Mexico	227	227	267	286	313
Puerto Rico	94	63	64	63	70
Trinidad & Tobago	12	14	13	15	17
USA	11,183	11,314	10,673	8,979	8,536

TABLE 73

NEW REGISTRATIONS
(unit: '000s)

SOUTH AMERICA

	1978	1979	1980	1981
Argentina	144.6	187.9	224.1	176.2
Brazil	836.4	863.9	818.3	460.0
Chile	36.2	39.0	63.0	91.5
Colombia	29.0	32.8	43.0	35.5
Uruguay	7.9	13.8	21.0	25.3
Venezuela	107.4	98.0	103.0	99.8

TABLE 74

NEW REGISTRATIONS
(unit: '000s)

NORTH AFRICA AND MIDDLE EAST

	1977	1978	1979	1980	1981
Iran	n/a	147.0	37.0	72.5	94.7
Iraq	n/a	5.1	25.1	45.9	54.9
Kuwait	46.7	49.1	47.1	36.2	31.4
Libya	46.3	50.5	55.0	19.2	75.0
Morocco	24.4	20.5	18.9	14.7	n/a
Saudi Arabia	n/a	134.0	134.0	171.0	147.0
UAR	20.0	23.3	27.0	29.6	29.9
Tunisia	3.5	4.3	3.9	—	—

TABLE 75

NEW REGISTRATIONS
(unit: '000s)

AFRICA

	1977	1978	1979	1980	1981
Benin	0.9	1.0	1.0		
Botswana	0.4	1.5	1.8		
Burundi	0.4	0.9	0.8		
Cameroon	5.5	6.5	6.0		
Central AR	0.6	0.7	0.5		
Chad	0.3	0.4	0.1		
Congo	1.4	1.3	1.4		
Egypt	25.5	20.0	25.0	21.6	19.0
Ethiopia	1.0	0.7	0.4		
Gambia	0.4	0.5	0.4		
Ghana	5.4	3.2	1.2		
Ivory Coast	12.8	15.4	14.6	16.4	12.4
Kenya	8.0	8.8	8.5	6.8	1.6
Liberia	2.8	3.0	2.4		
Madagascar	1.1	1.2	1.8		
Malawi	1.2	1.3	1.5	1.4	1.5
Mali	0.7	0.8	0.7		
Mauritius	3.6	1.1	0.6		
Niger	0.7	0.6	0.8		
Nigeria	91.0	67.4	62.3	108.1	137.0
Senegal	3.2	3.7	3.6		
South Africa	166.8	188.0	192.6	277.61	301.5
Sudan	2.3	2.9	1.5		
Tanzania	1.6	2.8	2.4		
Togo	2.6	2.5	2.1		
Uganda	3.1	0.8	0.4		
Upper Volta	0.8	0.9	0.7		
Zaire	3.1	2.1	1.0	1.3	1.8
Zambia	2.0	0.9	2.0	2.1	2.2

TABLE 76

NEW REGISTRATIONS
(unit: '000s)

FAR EAST

	1977	1978	1979	1980	1981
Hong Kong	22.5	24.4	27.6	33.9	28.0
India	38.0	35.0	29.6	31.0	32.0
Indonesia	18.0	19.1	18.0	34.0	37.0
Japan	2,500.1	2,856.7	3,036.9	2,854.2	2,866.9
Korea, South	53.5	69.2	86.6	45.0	50.6
Malaysia	56.0	75.4	70.1	97.3	100.0
Pakistan	12.6	13.2	11.7	13.3	7.2
Philippines	34.5	35.3	35.1	30.4	29.6
Singapore	15.3	18.7	25.0	30.8	
Taiwan	50.0	57.0	75.0	70.3	98.5
Thailand	26.5	27.2	25.4	22.6	30.0

TABLE 77

NEW REGISTRATIONS
(unit: '000s)

OCEANIA

	1977	1978	1979	1980	1981
Australia	430.4	441.5	460.6	450.2	453.8
Fiji	1.6	1.3	1.5	1.5	1.8
New Zealand	61.8	67.1	70.8	78.4	91.4
Papua New Guinea	3.0	2.8	2.8	2.7	2.6

TABLE 78

NEW CAR REGISTRATIONS IN AUSTRIA
(Units)

	1981
Volkswagen	36,256
Opel	21,436
Ford	17,435
Mazda	17,383
Datsun	10,826
Audi	7,167
Other	88,156
TOTAL	198,659

Source : OSZ

TABLE 79

NEW CAR REGISTRATIONS IN BELGIUM 1980/1981
(Units)

	1980	1981
Peugeot/Citroen/Talbot	63,049	49,058
VW Audi NSU	45,079	46,214
General Motors	41,034	38,190
Toyota	37,936	24,789
Renault	35,878	30,653
Ford	33,567	28,975
Other	142,697	133,121
TOTAL	399,240	351,000

Source : National Statistical Office

TABLE 80

NEW CAR REGISTRATIONS IN FRANCE 1980/1981
(Units)

	1980	1981
Renault	758,767	712,667
Citroen	270,983	260,286
Peugeot	293,461	256,287
Talbot	112,776	84,920
Volkswagen	75,727	101,929
Ford	68,439	101,336
Fiat	53,147	64,842
Opel	32,627	34,000
Alfa-Romeo	25,380	24,923
BMW	17,239	24,521
BL	21,282	20,936
Audi	17,455	20,283
Lada	13,069	19,324
Other	112,850	108,572
TOTAL	1,873,202	1,834,826

Source : l'Argus

TABLE 81

NEW CAR REGISTRATIONS IN ITALY 1979/1980
(Units)

	1979	1980
Fiat	641,967	654,972
Renault	121,041	160,138
Alfa Romeo	106,074	108,161
Citroen*	68,163	80,245
Ford	71,430	73,982
Volkswagen	56,431	67,126
Autobianchi	60,386	58,371
Simca	55,388	57,516
Opel	49,314	52,038
Other	166,845	217,694
TOTAL	1,397,039	1,530,243

Source : Anfia

TABLE 82

NEW CAR REGISTRATIONS IN THE NETHERLANDS 1979/1980
(Units)

	1979	1980
General Motors	92,073	69,032
Ford	63,879	41,044
Volkswagen	51,060	39,447
Renault	50,173	39,304
Toyota	26,076	27,100
Honda	21,086	24,923
Datsun	27,245	23,704
Peugeot	37,988	22,365
Citroen	27,574	22,019
Mitsubishi	15,736	21,460
Volvo	27,194	19,215
Others	134,975	100,463
TOTAL	575,059	450,076

Source : RAI

TABLE 83

**NEW CAR REGISTRATIONS IN NORWAY 1980/1981
(Units)**

	1980	1981
Ford	11,999	16,329
Mazda	11,434	11,948
Opel	9,910	13,401
Datsun	8,320	7,746
Toyota	8,226	7,051
VW	7,007	8,660
Volvo	6,936	7,083
Others	31,718	32,452
TOTAL	95,550	104,670

Source : CBS

TABLE 84

NEW CAR REGISTRATIONS IN SPAIN 1980/1981
(Units)

	1980	1981
Fasa Renault	215,773	185,010
Seat	141,921	125,722
Citroen	69,413	53,304
Ford	57,797	56,705
Talbot	57,097	54,221
TOTAL	542,001	474,962

Source : Confemetal

TABLE 85

**NEW CAR REGISTRATIONS IN SWEDEN 1980/1981
(Units)**

	1980	1981
Volvo	50,547	49,766
Saab	27,619	26,741
Volkswagen	18,683	20,002
Ford	16,109	21,128
Opel	17,409	15,913
Mazda	8,392	9,439
Other	53,829	45,533
TOTAL	192,588	188,522

Source : AB Bilstatisik

TABLE 86

NEW CAR REGISTRATIONS IN THE UNITED KINGDOM 1980/1981
(Units)

	1980	1981
BL	275,618	285,071
Ford	464,706	459,365
Vauxhall	109,218	107,572
Datsun	91,893	88,209
Talbot	90,874	68,048
Renault	88,343	72,041
VW/Audi	68,285	80,221
Fiat	45,267	55,505
Volvo	38,283	44,558
Toyota	34,167	23,405
Citroen	27,006	27,395
Peugeot	24,333	17,805
Honda	22,760	15,774
Other	133,008	139,653
TOTAL	1,513,761	1,484,622

TABLE 87

NEW CAR REGISTRATIONS IN WEST GERMANY 1980/1981
(Units)

	1980	1981
Volkswagen	526,368	557,163
Opel	402,015	370,285
Ford	250,630	272,389
Daimler-Benz	249,249	245,927
Audi	209,741	151,144
BMW	138,928	133,899
Renault	113,591	100,291
Fiat	79,229	93,620
Toyota	58,893	47,214
Nissan	51,503	44,722
Citroen	46,891	44,594
Toyo Kogyo	46,727	44,143
Mitsubishi	41,605	43,815
Honda	43,051	35,226
Other	167,766	145,903
TOTAL	2,426,187	2,330,335

Source : VDA

TABLE 88

NEW CAR REGISTRATIONS IN CANADA 1980/1981
(Units)

	1980	1981
General Motors	458,233	387,268
Ford	160,491	179,400
Chrysler	122,658	140,212
Honda	44,145	26,243
Toyota	37,659	13,205
Datsun	24,222	14,780
American Motors	22,895	17,713
Volkswagen	21,837	22,248
Other	39,860	37,022
TOTAL	932,000	838,091

Source : MVMA (Canada)

TABLE 89

NEW CAR REGISTRATIONS IN USA 1980/1981
(Units)

	1980	1981
General Motors	4,116,482	3,796,696
Ford	1,475,232	1,380,600
Chrysler	660,017	729,873
American Motors	149,438	136,682
Other	2,578,025	2,492,015
TOTAL	8,979,194	8,535,866

Source : MVMA (USA)

TABLE 90

SOUTH AFRICA : RETAIL SALES OF PASSENGER CARS 1980/1981
(Units)

	1980	1981
Volkswagen	55,186	51,426
Sigma Motor	55,176	50,866
Ford	41,442	50,460
Toyota	30,541	46,185
General Motors	27,371	33,204
Datsun-Nissan	30,551	29,951
Other	36,791	39,436
TOTAL	277,058	301,528

Source : National Association of Automobile Manufacturers

TABLE 91

**AUSTRALIA : RETAIL SALES OF PASSENGER CARS 1980/1981
(Units)**

	1980	1981
General Motors	110,822	109,405
Ford	89,622	104,362
Toyota	60,285	55,359
Mitsubishi	58,432	56,842
Datsun	52,434	56,205
Other	78,640	71,606
TOTAL	450,235	453,779

Source : Federal Chamber of Automotive Industries

TABLE 92

NEW ZEALAND : RETAIL SALES OF PASSENGER CARS 1980/1981
(Units)

	1980	1981
Mitsubishi	13,662	16,920
Toyota	12,374	13,123
Ford UK	11,875	8,881
Honda	7,799	11,068
Holden Australia	7,033	8,387
Nissan/Datsun	5,800	7,335
Other	19,829	25,659
TOTAL	78,372	91,373

Source : NZ Motor Trade Federation

TABLE 93

FORECASTS OF PASSENGER CAR SALES IN WESTERN EUROPE (1980-1990)
(Units)

	Total Park	New Registrations	Retired Cars	Used Imports
1980	102,628	9,894	6,645	22
1981	105,899	9,862	6,657	26
1982	109,130	10,813	7,328	28
1983	112,642	11,114	7,697	30
1984	116,089	11,403	8,076	32
1985	119,448	11,681	8,474	36
1986	122,691	11,938	8,849	38
1987	125,819	12,194	9,245	40
1988	128,807	12,449	9,614	41
1989	131,683	12,694	9,959	42
1990	134,460	12,938	10,349	43

Source : GM

APPENDIX B

Guide to Further Reading

I General background

Sources to consult for data showing the car industry in relation to all other industries are, for industrial statistics, the UNIDO *World Industry in 1982* and subsequent biennial issues (published by the United Nations in New York); for trade data, GATT, *International Trade 1980/81* and subsequent issues (published by GATT in Geneva) and IMF sources such as the annual *World Economic Outlook* (published by the IMF in Washington DC). Recent special studies which have referred to the car industry include the IMF's "Trade Policy Developments in Industrial Countries", by S.J. Anjaria et al (occasional Paper no.5), Washington DC, 1981; and *Employment, Trade and North-South Cooperation* (ILO: Geneva, 1981), edited by G.Renshaw. An annual statistical review is compiled by the Society of Motor Manufacturers and Traders, and is known as *The Motor Industry of Great Britain.* This contains an exhaustive survey of the British industry and a great deal of foreign data too.

Various other publications include statistics on production, external trade, circulation, and new registrations, although the figures vary and information on many countries is patchy. As a rule of thumb, the nearer the source to the country concerned, the more reliable the figures are likely to be, and the best figures are published by the statistical offices and motor trade organisations in the countries concerned.

Useful annual surveys include *The World Automotive Market* published by Automobile International (USA) which contains figures on car production and circulation in most countries. Similar coverage is offered by the French motor trade journal, *l'Argus* in a special June/July issue every year. European countries are covered by the Italian association *Anfia* in a monthly bulletin, while African countries are surveyed by *l'Automobile Outre-Mer.*

Statistics on new car sales or new registrations are harder to find. The only general source is *World Motor Vehicle Data* published annually by the Motor Vehicle Manufacturers Association of the United States. Naturally all the above publications are covered by normal copyright regulations.

II Car industry studies

Recent books on the car industry include G.Maxcy, *The Multinational Motor Industry* (London: Croom Helm, 1981), which is particularly strong on the history of the industry; D.T.Jones, *Maturity and Crisis in the European Car Industry: Structural Change* and Public Policy (Sussex University European Research Centre, 1981); K.Bhaskar *The Future of the World Motor Industry* (London: Kogan Page, 1980); and UNIDO, *The Manufacturing of Low-cost Vehicles in Developing Countries* (UN: New York, 1978). Publications which deal with themes of importance to the industry include L.R.Brown et al, "The Future of the Automobile in an Oil-short World" (Worldwatch Institute paper 32, Washington DC, 1979); and the larger study, mentioned in the text, from which it is drawn; W.J.Abernathy's *The Productivity Dilemma: Roadblock to Innovation in the Automobile Industry* (Johns Hopkins Press, 1978), which includes an exhaustive survey of the US firms' problems in cutting unit costs; and D.H. Ginsburg and W.J.Abernathy, *Government, Technology and the Future of the Automobile* (McGraw-Hill, New York, 1980).

A readable account of the development of a new model within a multinational producer is Edouard Seidler's *Let's Call It Fiesta: The Auto-Biography of Ford's Project Bobcat (Edita, Lausanne, 1976).*

III The Trade Press

Among the many journals and magazines which cover the car industry are *Ward's Auto World,* published monthly from Detroit; *Automotive News,* published weekly from Detroit; and, in Britain, such magazines as *Motor* and *Autocar.*

DATE DUE

MAR 26 '84		